Human–Computer Interaction Series

Editors-in-chief

Desney Tan, Microsoft Research, USA

Jean Vanderdonckt, Université catholique de Louvain, Belgium

HCI is a multidisciplinary field focused on human aspects of the development of computer technology. As computer-based technology becomes increasingly pervasive – not just in developed countries, but worldwide – the need to take a human-centered approach in the design and development of this technology becomes ever more important. For roughly 30 years now, researchers and practitioners in computational and behavioral sciences have worked to identify theory and practice that influences the direction of these technologies, and this diverse work makes up the field of human-computer interaction. Broadly speaking it includes the study of what technology might be able to do for people and how people might interact with the technology. The HCI series publishes books that advance the science and technology of developing systems which are both effective and satisfying for people in a wide variety of contexts. Titles focus on theoretical perspectives (such as formal approaches drawn from a variety of behavioral sciences), practical approaches (such as the techniques for effectively integrating user needs in system development), and social issues (such as the determinants of utility, usability and acceptability).

Titles published within the Human–Computer Interaction Series are included in Thomson Reuters' Book Citation Index, The DBLP Computer Science Bibliography and The HCI Bibliography.

More information about this series at http://www.springer.com/series/6033

John Waterworth • Kei Hoshi

Human-Experiential Design of Presence in Everyday Blended Reality

Living in the Here and Now

 Springer

John Waterworth
Department of Informatics
Umeå University
Umeå, Sweden

Kei Hoshi
School of Art, Architecture and Design
University of South Australia
Adelaide, Australia

ISSN 1571-5035
Human–Computer Interaction Series
ISBN 978-3-319-30332-1   ISBN 978-3-319-30334-5   (eBook)
DOI 10.1007/978-3-319-30334-5

Library of Congress Control Number: 2016937419

Printed on acid-free paper

This Springer imprint is published by Springer Nature
The registered company is Springer International Publishing AG Switzerland

Duality is an essential, isn't it? So long as there is myself *and* the other.

> *(Ursula LeGuin – The Left Hand of Darkness (1969).)*

Contents

List of Figures

List of Tables

Part I
Living in Mixed Reality

In this Part we start the book with a description of the unevenly mixed realities with which we are faced in everyday life, and with which we all deal in our work, and in our social and private lives. The difficulties inherent in functioning in these mixed informational spaces are described in terms of our inability to form a coherent sense of the presence within them. In Chap. 1, we discuss the importance of feeling present in the world around us, whether this is physical, virtual or, as is now commonplace, a mixture of the two, and introduce the idea of blended reality spaces The problems inherent in existing design approaches in addressing these issues are then examined in detail in Chap. 2.

Chapter 1
Introduction: Divided Presence in Mixed Reality

Abstract This chapter introduces the problems we all face in functioning within mixed realities, where our attention and other cognitive resources are often split between dealing with the physical world in which we are located and interacting with the digital which is ever more pervasively a part of almost everything we do. We discuss the nature of the sense of presence in the physical world and the digital world, and how they currently interfere with each other, stressing the discontinuities in communicational context between the two. We then briefly introduce the idea of blended reality spaces, which we propose as an answer to some of the problems of functioning in our current unevenly mixed reality, and in which we can experience a sense of presence integrated across the physical/digital divide.

Introduction

Technology is constantly changing, but people remain the same. This is the fundamental problem in designing human-computer interfaces and modes of interaction (HCI) for the ever-changing devices and systems with which and through which we work, play and live. But this also provides the opportunity to develop an approach to design that addresses the unchanging characteristics of the people interacting with the technology, and that is what we describe in this book. In it, we focus on two key aspects of people: how they make sense (of things, of situations, of language) and how they know what to make sense of (how they identify and act on what is in their here and now).

The first characteristic that we consider is the universal primitives underlying the way people understand things, events, relationships – and information generally. Because we are all embodied biological beings, meaning ultimately resides in bodily experiences. Our bodies and minds have evolved to act in the physical world, and how we are able to understand any information is derived from that. If we design for this embodiment, understandability should follow. And since we all share the same evolutionary history and hence, bodily structures and potential for experiences, we share the same primitives for understanding information. This is what makes social

© Springer International Publishing Switzerland 2016
J. Waterworth, K. Hoshi, *Human-Experiential Design of Presence in Everyday Blended Reality*, Human–Computer Interaction Series,
DOI 10.1007/978-3-319-30334-5_1

interaction possible. If we design for embodiment in the right way, the potential for shared understanding should also follow, even between people who exist in different contexts.

The second characteristic that we will consider in the book also draws on our embodied nature. This is our evolved *sense of presence*, which makes it possible for us to carry out our intentions and act in the world in which we currently find ourselves – whether this is physical, digital, or a mixture of the two. Together, these two aspects form the basis for what we call *human-experiential design.* Before delving more deeply into these two aspects of our design approach, we highlight below some features of the problems and opportunities that HCI design faces.

Through the ever-increasing proliferation of communication technologies, we all live in a variety of mixed realities formed from both the physical world and a virtual world of digitized information. We take with us mobile communication devices, and use them as we move through the physical world. While we are physically in one place, we are often mentally in another, or more than one other place, as we check e-mail or chat or chat with text or simply talk to other people in other places as we walk around, or eat or travel in vehicles. Increasingly, the devices that accompany us know where they are and can provide us with location relevant information, including the location of other people we may know. Increasingly, though still to a much lesser extent, the physical environments we move through are also equipped with embedded sensors, that can detect our presence, and adaptive displays, that can provide us with contingent information that is more or less relevant to our needs at that time and place.

This is the kind of mixed reality in which we all live. It is designed, but only in a piece-meal fashion. Parts of it are designed in detail, and some may be designed to work in combination, but overall the way the environment works and responds to us is not well adapted to supporting smooth transitions between the various functionalities of the many devices and systems we use and the different topographical and practical variations of the places in which we are physically located.

In this way, our lives have become spread between two intertwined, but not yet integrated, realities: the physical and the digital. Social interaction is similarly split, we struggle to manage our encounters with distant others brought to us via technology while simultaneously trying to fulfill the social expectations of those in our current physical vicinity. We seek to be psychologically and socially present both in the physical and the virtual world of networked communications. But since presence is an attention-demanding state (as we discuss later in this chapter), and because these worlds are mixed but not integrated, this is a troublesome and sometimes even dangerous task. Our sense of presence is split between the physical and digital worlds we inhabit. Moment by moment we must decide which reality to prioritize, and how and when to switch attention between the two becomes a major concern.

Blended (rather than mixed) reality (and which has also been termed "inter-reality" and "integral reality" – see, for example, Gaggioli et al. 2011) has been proposed as the answer to the dilemma of split presence inherent in mixed realities.

If only the physical/social world in which our bodies are located and the virtual world of digital information and communication could somehow be blended into one seamless reality. In this blend of the digital and the physical we would experience an integrated and unitary sense of presence. We would be able to function smoothly and effortlessly and enjoy the best of both worlds. But how can this be done? That is the main question we address throughout the book.

In the remainder of this chapter we discuss the nature of the sense of presence in the physical and the digital world, and how they can interfere with each other, stressing the discontinuities in communicational context between the two. We provide examples of the problems of this discontinuity and its effects in different everyday settings. We then introduce the idea of blended reality spaces, as an answer to problems of functioning in our current unevenly mixed realities.

Feeling Present in Mixed Reality

Presence and Mediated Presence

We define presence as *the feeling of being located in a perceptible external world around the self* (Waterworth et al. 2015). We see this as a universal animal faculty that allows an organism to distinguish the self from the non-self – what is part of the organism and what is not. This is a fundamental neurological ability supporting, amongst other activities, feeding, locomotion, sexual reproduction, and homeostasis. Its roots lie in proprioception and adaptive movement relative to the world around the organism.

Through evolution, animals gradually acquired the capacity to form internal representations of situations and things that are not physically present in their surroundings. This ability supports a range of intelligent behaviours, not least forming and mentally running future plans of possible actions, often based on remembered and selected aspects of earlier behaviour. In humans, a calibrated sense of presence has evolved to allow us to identify when and to what extent we are dealing with internal representations of past or possible future events as compared to when we are dealing with current events actually happening in our present environment (see Waterworth et al. 2010, 2015, for more details).

As thinking organisms, people routinely deal with two kinds of information, the concrete and the abstract. By definition, concrete information is in a form that can be dealt with directly via the perceptual-motor systems; it includes information coming from the world around us, and it gives rise to the sense of presence. Concrete information is realized *as the world* or, through digital technology as *a (virtual) world* that we experience as existing outside our minds. As far as out sense of presence is concerned, there is no difference between a fully convincing immersive virtual reality (VR) and the physical world. Mediated presence, as it is often called, is no different from the point of view of the organism from physical presence (Waterworth et al. 2010).

Presence is experienced strongly when we mostly attend to the currently present environment within and around the body (Waterworth and Waterworth 2001). The capacity we have for such attention depends on the amount of abstract conceptual processing a situation demands, as well as out own state of mental activation, because the capacity of our attention is strictly limited (see, e.g., Lavie et al. 2004; Lavie 2005). As we process more abstract, conceptual information we can consciously sample fewer concrete aspects of the present situation, and so our sense of presence diminishes and we become relatively *absent* (Waterworth and Waterworth 2001; Waterworth et al. 2010), in a state of being mentally removed from the world around us – whether this is physical or virtual.

We need to understand this presence-absence distinction if we are to understand how a digital virtual reality can evoke a coherent sense of presence, and why many mixed realities do not. Velmans (2000) describes how "What we normally call the 'physical world' just is what we experience. There is no additional experience of the world 'in the mind or brain'". Physical things are experienced as outside the body, in the external world, a process that Velmans calls "perceptual projection". But, as he further points out "We also have 'inner' experiences such as verbal thoughts, images, feelings of knowing, experienced desires, and so on" and "they are reflexively experienced to be roughly where they are (in the head or brain)" (Velmans 2000, p. 110). Perceptual projection can occurs in response to both physical reality and virtual reality. As Velmans states: "Virtual reality systems in which one *appears* to interact with a (virtual) three-dimensional world in the absence of an *actual* (corresponding) world provide one of the best demonstrations of perceptual projection in action" (Velmans 2000, p. 231). Perceptual projection underlies our definition of presence as the feeling of being in an external (to the body) world, whereas absence is the feeling of being in an internal world, a world 'in the head'.

The distinction between internally- and externally-generated worlds becomes clear if we consider the difference between reading a gripping novel and acting in a convincing VR. The world of the novel is depicted in abstract form – the symbols of textual language printed on a page or presented on a screen. We must do conceptual work to realize this world in our minds. A VR, in contrast, is depicted in a concrete form, and can be experienced in the ideal case without extra conceptual work and by exactly the same perceptual processes we draw on to interact with the physical world. Most importantly, virtual realities and physical realities can be *shared*. Other things being equal, a specific physical place that I visit is the same place when you visit it (event though your experience there will be somewhat different) and, in the same way, a specific virtual reality that I enter is the same one that you enter. We may meet each other in a virtual reality or in a physical place.

In contrast, the world I realize in my head when I read a novel is not the same as the one you realize, though it will have some similarities. It makes no sense to say that I will meet you in a place depicted in a novel. We can share external worlds in which we feel present, but we cannot share imagined worlds in the same way. Thus media form determines the extent to which information is realized externally, and so is sharable, or internally (Waterworth et al. 2015). The key formal requirement for mediated presence to occur is that information is presented in a concrete form that an observer can make sense of intuitively (and literally, through sensations of the body), rather than having to think about. The result is the feeling of being in an external world, of presence.

Referring back to the roots of the feeling of presence, Waterworth and Waterworth (2010) propose that when we experience strong mediated presence, we experience that the technology has become part of the self, and the mediated reality to which we are attending becomes an integrated part of the non-self, the world around the self. When this happens, in the same way as when we act directly in the physical world, there is no additional conscious effort of access to information presented in a medium, nor is there an extra effort of action to respond in the mediated environment. This is the ideal case of human-computer interaction.

Fragmented Presence in Mixed Reality

As we have seen, and especially thanks to the proliferation of mobile devices and distributed systems, we often interact with both the physical world in which we are located and with the digital world of phone calls, text messages and chats, tweets, uploaded images and news feeds. Some of these will evoke presence in the medium, to a greater or lesser extent depending on the form in which they are transmitted, but others will generate mental absence as we attend to them. In current mixed realities, a sense of presence in the physical world is often in competition with both presence and absence in the virtual world of the digital.

Cognitive load will tend to be inversely related to the level of presence experienced, since it is a reflection of the abstractness of a communicative medium. The locus of attention is another important factor (Waterworth and Waterworth 2001). A concrete, perceptual presentation of information will interfere less with a other more abstract task than an abstract description. While high cognitive loads will interfere more with other types of attention-demanding task than will low cognitive loads, two perceptual (and thus potentially presence-evoking) tasks may strongly interfere with each other even though each imposes a relatively low cognitive load. If the individual is already focusing his or her attention on the external world, as when driving, there will be a conflict between one perceptual task (driving) and another (say, looking at a navigation system display). In short, our sense of presence in current mixed realities is complex and fragmented.

Another significant feature of digital communications is their frequent lack of symmetry. The different parties in an interaction will often be in different kinds of physical and/or digital situation, with very different characteristics. In two completely different situations the same message may be experienced in very different ways. At one end of a conversation, a person may be ready and able to be fully immersed in the communicative medium. At the other, the would-be communicator may have restricted attention, or bandwidth, or both, to devote to the interaction. A relatively abstract form of communication may also be a matter of choice. In today's society people often choose to chat with text rather than speaking to someone else with their voice. This may be for economic reasons, or to reduce memory load; but it may also be to reduce the sense of presence inherent in dealing with the communication.

Waterworth and Waterworth (2006), give the example of one person waiting for a flight, who receives a text message from a loved one. She has plenty of time to compose a heartfelt reply, but starts her message with a playfully provocative remark. As she is about to respond further, it is announced that her flight is actually at a different gate, quite some distance away. She will have to move quickly if she is to get to the gate on time, and so she has no time to finish the text exchange as intended, not even time to explain her current, changed situation. She sends the partially composed message anyway, because she was expected to do so, and runs to the newly announced gate. But the receiver, unaware of the context in which the message was composed, completely misunderstands the sender's intent and is upset by its tone and brevity.

A communication medium with greater presence for both parties might have made the problem less likely to arise although. By definition, more presence evoked by a communication form means that more information about the present situation external to the sender is being transmitted. In a phone message, for example, the sender could explain the situation more quickly, while dashing to the correct location. And the sender would also receive indications of the sender's true state, through paralinguistic cues such as breathing style, intonation, pitch and so on, as well as acoustic information from the surroundings. If video capability is also available, this tendency might be further enhanced, by showing facial expression, visual features of the surroundings, and so on.

Contextual factors will affect a person's state. One of the best ways of tracking context is through tracking a person's state, although without also tracking physical context this is open to misinterpretation. A person running to a departure gate at an airport needs primarily to attend to physical reality, but may yet be talking or texting a distant other person. This person may be sitting in an armchair, sipping a cup of coffee, willing and able to be immersed in the caller's communication. State-sensitive communication devices would be one way to cater for the fact that different individuals will often have the possibility for different levels of presence in different situations. People may also want to customise the level of concreteness – and hence potential for presence – of their communications according to the situation or the identity of the person they are communicating with. I may prefer to send a text than speak to a certain other person, and even if the situation makes it difficult to type, current technology allows my speech to be presented as text if I so choose.

Issues of communicational asymmetry described above point to a *contextual reality gap* between the parties, a gap that makes communication difficult when one, but not the other, is experiencing fragmented presence in a mixed reality. We discuss gaps in contextual reality, and our approach to dealing with them in detail, in Chap. 5. In the remainder of this chapter, we briefly summarise our approach and the scope of the rest of the book.

Integrated Presence in Blended Reality Spaces

Given the problematic nature of mixed reality, the need for blended reality spaces is clear. We address the problem of designing them by suggesting an approach rooted in a return to first principles of how people understand the world, consciously and unconsciously, and how this determines the way they think, act, an communicate. This, combined with a consideration of factors affecting the experience of presence, is what we call *human-experiential design*. Our aim is to support efforts to create the ideal HCI, where there is no extra effort of access to information not effort of action in the world, even though we are located in a reality that combines physical and digital elements.

Human-experiential design is a response to the problems of existing approaches to design, which are outlined in Chap. 2. It is based in the cognitive principles of human understanding; specifically, metaphorical projection and blending theory. What this approach brings to the design of blended reality spaces is, initially, the insight that successful design – not least human-computer interaction design – depends on the development and cognitive assimilation of appropriate *blends*.

A blend combines at least two existing conceptual spaces to become a new thing in itself, understood and used almost unconsciously in the lives of users. For example, *cutting and pasting* with a digital tool has become a thing in itself, but was originally designed and understood on the basis of two conceptual spaces: one composed of paper, paste pots and scissors; the other of computers able to take in information from a source, store it, and output it as required. The new blend is no longer thought of, experienced or used as a combination of two domains, but as a single entity – *cutting and pasting*. This entity is then available as an input space to further blended, in which *cutting and pasting* can be combined with another conceptual space, such as composing music. Chapter 3 describes this design approach in detail, with a particular focus on the importance of metaphor and blends in HCI design.

Human-experiential design is also a response to the needs of people for a way of balancing their physical and communicational needs in a new, emerging world. These problems of design include a mismatch between the concerns of technologies versus the concerns of people. Human-experiential design provides a way to bridge contextual gaps in understanding, for example between young and old, between here and there, and between the technologically savvy and the relatively naïve. It is a way designing blends of the physical and virtual in which contextual gaps are bridged and we can feel a unitary sense of being present.

Chapters 4 and 5 describe how human-experiential design takes the existing blending approach to HCI design a step further by applying it to the design of combinations of physical and digital realities, making it possible to bridge *contextual reality gaps* between distant participants in an interaction. In this process, what were previously understood and used as mixed realities become transformed into blended reality spaces. For example, sending text messages on a mobile phone while driving is a challenging, hazardous, often illegal and yet not uncommon activity in modern life. Applying human-experiential design to this case would in principle enable the writer/driver to both communicate (in digital space) and control the vehicle (in physical space) as an integrated activity within a blended reality space.

Chapters 6 and 7 of the book provides case histories and scenarios of real life situations that can be seen as early examples of physical/digital blending, bringing out in a practical way the value of human-experiential design. We conclude the book with speculations about further developments and provide a vision of a future where we all live and function in a blended reality that is both physical and digital.

Human-experiential design of physical-digital materials and environments has the potential to impact on our lives in several different but ultimately interrelated ways:

- **Firstly,** our mental activities will be changed along with some of the ways in which we carry out our intentions. An integrated sense of physical/mediated presence can potentially provide a smoother link between our intentions and actions in mixed reality.
- Secondly, the way in which we perceive and function with our bodies – our sense of our own embodiment – is changed when we perceive ourselves acting from the altered perspectives provided by technology. Depending on how altered embodiment is designed, this can impede or assist us in dealing with mixed realities.
- Thirdly, the widespread transformation of our social lives with technology is ongoing and ever expanding. This can lead to a reduction in our sense of the reality of others, but also to situations in which we share more information with others than ever before, and in ways that were previously impossible. How and in what respects we are aware of others should depend on the contextual situation in which we find ourselves.
- Finally, the digital transformation of physical places is a growing product of designed mixed reality spaces, both through architectural installations and through mobile and wearable devices.

We have suggested that the physical/social world in which our bodies are located and the virtual world of digital information and communication at a distance should somehow be blended into one seamless reality, so that we can function smoothly and effortlessly and enjoy the best of both worlds. We have the technical means, but how can such a smooth blending be achieved? Can we design truly blended reality spaces, and how might we go about doing that?

First, we have to recognize the problems with existing design approaches.

References

Gaggioli A, Raspelli S, Grassi A, Pallavicini F, Cipresso P, Wiederhold BK, Riva G (2011) Ubiquitous health in practice: the interreality paradigm. Stud Health Technol Inform 163:185–191

Lavie N (2005) Distracted and confused?: selective attention under load. Trends Cogn Sci 9(2): 75–82

Lavie N, Hirst A, De Fockert J, Viding E (2004) Load theory of selective attention and cognitive control. J Exp Psychol Gen 133(3):399–354

Velmans M (2000) Understanding consciousness. Routledge/Psychology Press, London

Waterworth EL, Waterworth JA (2001) Focus, locus and sensus: the 3 dimensions of virtual experience. Cyberpsychol Behav 4(2):203–214

Waterworth JA, Waterworth EL (2006) Presence as a dimension of communication: context of use and the person. In: Riva G, Anguera MT, Wiederhold BK, Mantovani F (eds) From communication to presence: cognition, emotions and culture towards the ultimate communicative experience (Festschrift in honor of Luigi Anolli). IOS Press, Amsterdam

Waterworth EL, Waterworth JA (2010) Mediated presence in the future. In: Bracken CC, Skalski PD (eds) Immersed in media: telepresence in everyday life. Routledge, Taylor & Francis Group, New York, pp 183–196

Waterworth JA, Waterworth EL, Mantovani F, Riva G (2010) On feeling (the) present. J Conscious Stud 17(1–2):167–188

Waterworth JA, Waterworth EL, Riva G, Mantovani F (2015) Presence: form, content and consciousness. In: Lombard M, Biocca F, Freeman J, IJsselsteijn W, Schaevitz RJ (eds) Immersed in media: telepresence theory, measurement & technology. Springer International Publishing, Switzerland. ISBN: 978-3-319-10189-7

Chapter 2
The Problems of Design

Abstract HCI design is difficult, partly because of the dichotomy between the concerns of people and the directives provided by newly available technologies. There is a tension between what the devices and systems can do (objectivity), and how we experience using them and living with them (subjectively). A designer needs to know both what is technically possible, and how we think and act when our lives are mediated by technology. This chapter discusses a range of problems with the way design has been understood and is conducted. We see design as having the responsibility to ensure that people can fulfil themselves and act out their intentions in the world of things (including of technology). We raise several issues surrounding so-called human-centred design as a response to this concern, issues that we see as caused by three false dichotomies: (i) the 'cognition-action dichotomy', (ii) the 'human-user dichotomy', and (iii) the 'virtual-physical dichotomy'. The chapter also reframes the categorization of customers, users, persons and humans, allowing us to focus on new aspects of people as humans in design work.

Introduction

All HCI design is difficult, partly because of the dichotomy between the concerns of people and the directives provided by newly available technologies. There is a tension between what the devices and systems can do (objectivity), and how we experience using them and living with them (subjectively). Design as a discipline has been influenced by the basically mechanistic and dualistic worldview of the scientific tradition, by being seen as apart from this. From a Cartesian perspective, design in general is interpreted primarily as a way to create decoration to adorn the outer surface of things, to producing transitory 'feelings' without involving logical thinking. By this view, designing is seen as an activity drawing on with subjective sense experiences and imagination.

But if design is about touching people's heartstrings, it comes into being by way of a process that interweaves this sensitivity with the logic of properties of material and colours (which are subjective phenomena), functionalities and usability (which

© Springer International Publishing Switzerland 2016
J. Waterworth, K. Hoshi, *Human-Experiential Design of Presence in Everyday Blended Reality*, Human–Computer Interaction Series, DOI 10.1007/978-3-319-30334-5_2

are objective phenomena), amongst many other properties (Walls et al. 1992; Hevner et al. 2004). In other words, design implies that the senses and logic, the mind and the body, the surface and the structure affect each other.

Even though it is not really possible to dissociate them, we are familiar with thinking about the origin of things in terms of a fundamental dichotomy, as either subjective or objective. The liberal arts, visual arts, music and literature are essentially human activities that carry the assumption of subjectivity. On the other hand, in the more mechanistic objective view of the universe, the whole world is seen as a closed, material system that mechanically operates according to natural, physical laws. Although adopting the latter has brought us the apparent progress of recent technological change and economical opportunities (and pressures) into our lives, it has also produced a gap between the human scale of being and the industrial scale of production. That may be a sign of success for the human race as a whole (or not), but what have we lost in the process?

Even though human life is experientially delicate, aesthetical, the industrial scale and force of technological production exposes us to rapidly accelerating change. This gap between the human scale and industrial scale has the effect of replacing design's deeper potential role with that of a promotional and presentational tool for introducing the novel fruits that technology brings us. The subjective-objective dichotomy is one of several dichotomies that we touch on in this chapter (see Table 2.1).

The essence of a human being cannot be formalized. However, in our current recklessly progressive industrial era, human beings have been seen as formalized groups of user/customers with certain objective statistical characteristics. People struggle to understand and use computers, mobile phones and other embedded computing devices, whose designs are still largely based on a formalization of human understanding of the world in terms of explicit conceptual knowledge. Because of this, people often have to adapt themselves to the mediated computing environment (if they can), because human sensation and perception are essentially embodied and thus implicit phenomena.

The human being and the user/customer have been separated, in other words. The nature of actual human beings has been lost within formalized user/customer groups.

	Subjective	Objective
Table 2.1 Examples of dichotomies in design	Mind	Body
	Liberal arts	Natural sciences
	Human/person	User/customer
	Internal	External
	Implicit	Explicit
	Virtual	Physical
	Experiential	Practical
	Human-experiential design	User-experience design

Table 2.1 Examples of dichotomies in design

Even applied observation techniques used in recent design processes commonly see their subjects as people who use products in general, who tell stories as users, who use a particular product. The needs of human beings, and perhaps especially the vulnerable, the elderly and the socially handicapped, have become increasingly unsatisfied by the unbalanced environment created with mediating information technology. We believe that they should no longer be expected to tolerate the problems that much current design of technology brings (Waterworth et al. 2009a, b). We discuss some of these practical problems in more detail, as well as ways in which they can be addressed in Part III of the book.

The Cartesian mechanistic view underlying much of science has brought an undesirable gap between people and their increasingly technology-mediated environment. It seems that objectivism reigns supreme especially in science. When design is seen through a scientific lens, 'design science' becomes a blind acceptance of the objective position. In contrast, our view is that there is no absolute design science or designed products that reveal objective truths about the world. What is prominent and fair design in one culture is often poor design in another culture, even though they may make for successful business in both.

Objective Versus Subjective Views of Design

Design has often been viewed as a craft, as tacit, unknowable and experiential, and designers are viewed as subjective and not purely rational or objective - but this is mostly by people other than actual design practitioners. This subjective perspective can be summarized in the following points (taken from Lakoff and Johnson 1980, p. 188, summarized and modified). This is "*the myth of subjectivism*":

- Designers' senses and intuitions are their best guides for design activities. They rely on their senses and develop intuitions they must trust.
- Designers believe that feelings, aesthetic sensibilities, moral practice, and spiritual awareness are essential in human life, and are good design resources and practices.
- Art, music and poetry and so on put designers in touch with the more important reality of their feelings and intuitions. Designers gain this awareness through imagination rather than reason, rationality and objectivity.
- Designers use the language of the imagination for expressing the unique and most personally significant aspects of their experience. Ordinary explicit language is not suitable for matters of personal understanding.
- Designers believe that objectivity can be dangerous, because it misses what is most important and meaningful to individual people. Therefore, they believe that objectivity can be inhuman, and it is harmful for true 'human-centred' design.

In contrast, people who believe that science is absolute truth that can give a correct, definitive, and general account of reality through the application of scientific methodology, claim the following with respect to design. This is *"the myth of objectivism"*, summarized and modified (Lakoff and Johnson 1980, p. 186):

- To the extent that scientists are objective, science is rational. To the extent that designers are subjective, to design is irrational and is to give in to the emotions.
- Whereas scientists are objective, designers are subjective indulgers since they emphasize the importance of the personal point of view.
- Scientists are objective and always fair. Therefore they can avoid personal prejudice and a biased view of the external world.
- Science provides us with a methodology that allows us to be fair, understanding things from a universally valid and unbiased point of view. On the other hand, design relies on the personal judgments of a designer.
- Scientists deal with only objective knowledge that is absolute knowledge. They speak objective language that is clearly and precisely defined, that is straightforward and direct, and that can fit reality. Designers use poetic, fanciful, rhetorical, and figurative language in ways such that meanings are not clear and precise and do not fit reality in an obvious way.
- There is an objective reality, and scientists can say things that are objectively, absolutely, and unconditionally true and false about it. Illusions, errors of perception, errors of judgment, emotions, and personal and cultural biases are human error.
- Scientists believe that the world is made up of objects that have properties independent of any people or other beings that experience them. For example, a rock is a separate object and it is hard.
- Scientists believe that we obtain knowledge of the world by experiencing the objects in it and getting to know what properties the objects have and how these objects are related to one another. Therefore they believe that subjective thought and intuition can be dangerous, since they can be lead to losing touch with reality.

Viewed from these mythical perspectives, the position of science reflects the view that the external world needs to be understood so that humans can live properly in it. The position of design is focused on internal aspects of understanding the world. Designers intend to address what makes human life meaningful and worth living. On the other hand, the position of science says that, for example, the elements of the universe as separated from each other, divisible and wholly isolated.

The Cognition-Action Dichotomy

In his Discourse on Methods (1637), Descartes argued that we exist as thinking beings, different from brute animals. The world is made up of two separated substances; physical substances (bodies) and mental substances (minds). This Cartesian view underlies much of science, and has allowed vast areas of understanding of previously mysterious phenomena to develop and flourish. On the other hand, the dichotomy has brought undesirable effects, and is even reflected in HCI, in various aspects of so-called 'Human-centred design', as we shall see. It has made it extremely difficult to find a place in our views of human meaning and rationality for structures of imagination. As Johnson (1987, xxix) expressed it: "Imagination seems to exist in a no-man's-land between the clearly demarcated territories of reason and sensation."

Traditionally, HCI researchers have the assumption that the brain functions to construct and utilize representations of the world around us, via 'a model of the world' (Craik 1943; Reed 1996). The human organism must collect, collate, and interpret stimuli until it has an internal model of the world constructed by the brain (or mind), in order to let it send commands that will cause its body to behave in suitable ways. Several scholars and disciplines have argued against the limitations of this cognitivist view of HCI, as found in discussions in terms of augmented and mixed realities, tangible interaction, and situated action (e.g. Dourish 2001; Suchman 2007). We return to these later.

Lakoff refers to the view that the mind is a computer with biological hardware:

> the mind runs using programs essentially like those used in computers today and it may take input from the body and provide output to the body, but there is nonetheless a purely mental sphere of symbolic manipulation that can be characterized in terms of algorithms of the sort used in computer programs. (Lakoff 1987, p. 338)

Such mechanical systems all have one thing in common: They must have an external agency in order to let them act. Based on this assumption, it may be true that a tool is something that extends the action of workers. Therefore a tool, for example a computer, can do this only because workers and other sources of power bring it into action. Designers of interactive systems adopting this cognitivist view have tended to assume that every emergence of action/behaviour needs a stimulus either from outside the system or from inside. These are so-called reactive mechanisms based on external stimuli and instructive mechanisms based on internal stimuli or commands, according to some theories of ecological psychology (Reed 1996).

Whereas machines need a stimulus to bring them into action, animals are always active in whole or in part. We experientially know also that humans are always active and different from machines. And even though machines, tools and computers are not active in the way that animals are, interactive systems have been designed on the basis of modelling animal and human behaviour on mechanical principles. For example, Card et al. (1983) introduced the idea of a model human processor (MHP) in their GOMS (goals, operators, methods and selection rules) approach to understanding interaction. The MHP describes human behaviour in terms of memories, processors, their parameters and interconnections. It is supposed to be used for approximate prediction, such as the assumed information processing capacities of a person, gross behaviour, and user behaviour in HCI, by applying a simplified view of psychological theories and empirical data. The MHP can be said to be an integration of a set of memories and processors.

The MHP is composed of three subsystems that have their own memories and processors: the perceptual system, the cognitive system and the motor system. The perceptual system consists of two different image stores: an auditory image store and a visual image store. While it is being symbolically encoded, the output of the sensory system is retained. The cognitive system receives information symbolically coded from the perceptual system that contains the sensory image stores in its working memory and employs information previously stored in long-term memory to decide about how to react. The motor system then carries out the responses. There is a separate processor in each subsystem: a perceptual processor, a cognitive processor and a motor processor, which have a capacity for both serial and parallel processing.

The cognitivist view considers that users act rationally to obtain their goals. On this base, we can predict a user's behaviour by determining the user's goals, methods and operators and the constraints of the task. This has been formulated in the GOMS approach, which helps predict user's behaviour, based on the assumption that

> underlying the detailed behaviour of a particular user there are a small number of information processing operators, that the user's behavior is describable as a sequence of these, and that the time the user requires to act is the sum of the time of these individual operators. (Card et al. 1983, p. 139)

The GOMS model specifies the components that a user's cognitive structure is supposed to be composed of: a set of goals, a set of operators, a set of methods for attaining the goals, and a set of selection rules for choosing appropriate methods for goals. By this and similar approaches, HCI largely concerns itself with the complex environmental conditions in which humans are put into motion via stimuli (as inputs received by the brain). Their behaviours are responsive outputs generated by the nervous system. The human "operator" is essentially seen as a computing environment interacting with another, external computing environment.

We can find challenging and interesting applications for educational, medical and industrial usage designed on the basis of such basically mechanical principles, but many are not at all suitable for actual people, and especially not for people with special needs. People, as human beings, are forced to adapt to the external computing environment based on mechanistic principles, even though human behaviours can be seen instead as essentially a natural flow of action based on constant activity. In this kind of approach, design is rational to the extent that a designer is being objective.

The Human-User Dichotomy

HCI designers historically sought a new concept of "user interfaces", especially for office workers, since computer users were historically almost all office workers. The designers therefore tried to evoke explicitly people's knowledge of office work to help them understand the operation of the computer.

The typical design approach to HCI design used metaphor in order for users to understand how to use a computing system (Imaz and Benyon 2006; Waterworth et al. 2003). This encompasses what users feel, think, and are able to do as they interact, and has often been called *User-Experience Design* in the last few years.

The user-experience designer tries to help users' understand the system by adopting users' experience in another domain (Imaz and Benyon 2006; Waterworth et al. 2003) and applying it in design. Over the past 30 years or so, more and more interface designers have adopted this style. Recently it has been spreading to other devices such as mobile phones, digital cameras, audio-visual equipment, and most web sites used in everyday life.

But user-experience design is a very fuzzy concept and the term is used in many different ways. User experience design is supposed to be rooted from the principles of human-centred design as defined, for example, in ISO 13407 (1999). In essence, user-experience design conforms to human-centred design principles. Whereas human-centred design as defined in such standards largely focuses on traditional usability factors, recent user-experience design focuses more on factors relevant to affect, interpretation and meaning (Roto et al. 2011). Designers, especially user-experience designers, emphasize that user-experience design focuses on humans and their experiences with and of technology, not merely on using the technology. We can find a number of definitions of user experience design in academic papers (Alben 1996; Hassenzahl and Tranctinsky 2006; Sward and MacArthur 2007; Hekkert 2006; Hassenzahl 2008; Colbert 2005) and well-known websites such as www.nngroup.com (Nielsen-Norman Group); www.upassoc.org (Usability Professionals' Association); and www.interaction-design.org.

There are also other approaches to understanding user experience, such as co-experience, shared experience and group experience, which focus on the social aspects that are hypothesised as contributing to the construction of experience (Hassenzahl 2010). Since digital products, computers and mobile phones have become distributed almost everywhere, social and cultural aspects of design are becoming increasingly important. Recent approaches consider the situations in which experiences are constructively formed and where participants mutually create interpretations and meanings from everyday life contexts, thus allowing for co-evolution of designs with social practices (Battarbee 2003).

Even though there are many definitions of user-experience design, it is not easy to find any distinction made between being a user of technology and a human being. A user is typically conceived of as focused on foreground tasks through full access to a central display. The mouse is used as part of a two dimensional paradigm that assists with easy spatial navigation of the displayed contents, by clicking, dragging, selecting and operating on 2D graphical objects. Although this is in some ways a flexible approach, two-dimensional input-output interface is still limited when applied to many activities, for example face-to-face collaboration or in fundamentally distributed environments. People have again to adapt to the limited computing environment, which breaks their natural flow of action.

To define true human-centred design would be to give an answer to the question of who we are as humans. This assumes that we are not merely segmented customers or just users of technology, and much less are we predictable machines. Given the correct design approach, people need not – indeed should not – be aware of themselves as users. Design should aim to realize an ideal in which our activities are characterized by a natural flow of action, without any intrusions from technology. It is time to consider reframing audiences from users to humans. Human is a universal concept. It includes the young, the old, and those with special needs such as patients, elderly people and those with disabilities. In fact, all people, as human beings, have special needs. If we take this view seriously, how would 'users' be redefined?

Users and User-Centred Systems Design

According to the Oxford Dictionary of English (2003), A user is '*a person who uses or operates something.*' In computing, a user is a person who uses computer hardware/software or an Internet service. However, what do users actually do in their use of these artefacts/products?

As a term, User-Centred System Design (UCSD) was introduced by Donald Norman and Stephen Draper (1986), and reflected the already ongoing development of User Centred Design (UCD) in the 1980s. Keinonen (2008) states that: "UCD is a broad umbrella covering approaches such as traditional human factors and ergonomics, participatory design, human-centred design processes, usability measurements and inspections, and design for user experience" (p. 211). Humanistic roles of design were emphasized and widely brought over into the product development process, which became and remains a dominant subject in HCI. Later, the human-centred design concept was developed and applied to overcome the design weaknesses of software products with WIMP (windows, icons, menus, pointer) graphical user interfaces. The process contributed to the evolution of the standard WIMP interface and of the growth and success of consumer information technology in the market.

Since the advent of modern WIMP interfaces launched for ordinary people, and especially for the office work environment, computing for the masses has continued to grow. The domain of HCI has been continuously expanding into our everyday life. Using standard office type applications, such as word processors, databases, and spread sheets became a common part of our lives, even though people in everyday life are essentially not office workers. 'User', inheriting meaning from users in office settings, is still in the centre of the product development process as a guiding concept.

User-centred design approaches have been repeatedly emphasized in both design literature and practical development practices. There is also an ISO standard for the user-centred design process with an emphasis on user participation in the system development process (ISO 13407 1999). The standard provides guidance on "human-centred design activities throughout a development life cycle of computer-based interactive systems", but does not specify detailed methods and techniques. The usability, accessibility and understandability of the products have been improved by emphasizing user centredness, of listening to the user's voice.

Although there has been much improvement in these areas, the complexity of the products remains high. Even companies who claim to follow human-centred principles have released complex, confusing products. In both academia and industry, many disciplines and professionals use the terms user-centred and human-centred design without any clear distinction. In the domains of interaction design, HCI, and information systems design, many use such generic terms as human-centred computing (HCC), human-centred design (HCD), and human-centred systems (HCS) in a simplistic way without a common foundation of understanding (Bannon 2011).

In order to understand the complexity of users, applied user observation techniques based on working more closely with users have been introduced, such as ethnographic studies and participatory design. Interdisciplinary groups formed with such professionals as anthropologists, psychologists, and designers, are often involved in the development process. According to Mactavish (2009, p. 121), gathering quantitative data about user activity and behaviour (for recent products such as mobile phones, personal digital assistants, and various computer applications) includes formal study of task productivity based on learning time, task initiation time, task completion time, task completion success rate, operator error rate, error recovery tasks, error recovery time and so on. Researchers normally aggregate these data by direct observation or video capturing, logging data based on various interaction aspects, sometimes with biometric monitoring (Mactavish 2009).

Sato (2009, p. 30) characterises the knowledge cycle between artefact development and user. According to him, development groups generate knowledge by analysing users and usage of artefacts and embed it in future artefacts. Users also produce knowledge by using, reading and interpreting embedded knowledge in the artefacts, and understand the significance, meaning, and validity of using the artefact in various situations in their everyday life. What has been discussed in the recent user-centred design process exemplifies the knowledge cycle between artefact development and the user.

A user-centred design process can thus be seen as a process centring on the knowledge lifecycle that includes knowledge of use, knowledge of design and the user who generates knowledge through interpretation of embedded design knowledge in artefacts/products. It begins by observing the activities and interactions of users in a certain situation. Hence, users can be defined as; *people who have knowledge of use and generate knowledge relevant to artefacts/products in a knowledge lifecycle between user, artefact and artefact development.* User-centred design is a design activity based on the cycle of this mainly explicit knowledge of use.

In the process of practical design development, industry practitioners also use customer data for interpreting, understanding, and discovering customer value-based demands (Mello 2002). This enables companies to find not only new markets but also repeatable product life cycles and measurable product development cycles. Here, there is a simple question. Although 'user' can be defined, how can 'customer' be defined? What are the differences between users and customers in the information gathering process?

What Is a Customer?

In general, a customer is "*a person who buys goods or service from a shop or business*" (Oxford Dictionary of English 2003). 'A customer' more specifically refers to a current or potential buyer or user of the products of an individual or organization that is usually called the *supplier*, *seller*, or *vendor* through purchasing or renting goods or services. Depending on the industry, a customer may also be called a *client*, *buyer*, or *purchaser*. There is a place where buyer and seller meet, which refers to a set of potential customers, the 'market'. If buyer refers to a customer, then seller refers to a company/corporation. Organizations sometimes use terms and phrases such as "customer-oriented, customer-driven, listening to the voice of the customer, customer-centric, customer awareness, and customer retention" to emphasize that the customer and the market drive the business (Mello 2002, p. 4). This results in what is sometimes called 'customer-centred design'. Since industries often exploit user-centred design as a tool to get their own customers, 'customer' and 'user' have been frequently confused or used interchangeably.

A business strategy, regarded as essential for success in the market, is a plan of action designed to accomplish credible defined goals that generally include "sales volume, rate of growth, profit percentages, market share, and return on investment (ROI), among others" (Rosenzweig 2003, p. 1). These concepts help to understand a market rather than give an understanding of users and the usage of products. Markets can be represented accurately in terms of segments. The first task of a marketing group is to identify relevant market segments, which creates a framework for developing market strategy with segmentation variables such as "demographic, geographic, psychographic, product use and application so on" (Rosenzweig 2003, p. 3). Some may be defined as subsets of other variables. For example, the marketing people may segment the world in terms of country markets and then analyse each, using lifestyle variables.

In the segmentation process, human beings are formalized into customer groups. For example, according to Rosenzweig (2003), demographic segmentation categorises people using family income, age, sex, ethnicity, and education level as explanatory variables predicting differences in taste, buying behaviour, and consumption patterns (p. 3); while psychographic segmentation categorises consumer lifestyle according to parameters such as attitudes towards self, work, family and peer group identity (p. 4). There are a variety of techniques and methods, but they are all ways of formalization of human to customer. In such approaches, 'customer' is represented as an abstract person with objective statistical characteristics.

Human-Centred and Human-Experiential Design

We tend to believe that most of our actions are carried out consciously. It is, however, our unconscious behaviour that preserves the natural flow of action in many situations. We become harmonized to things that all of us end up doing without really thinking. For example, in specific situations, placing something for convenience, holding hands to ones forehead because of blinding sunlight, and bringing up a cool canned drink to ones cheek are universal and instinctive, drawing on experiences with mind, body, and environment so embodied that they are largely unconscious. According to Suri (2005, p. 164), "this awareness is evident from our actions, even when we are not conscious of them. These are unconscious behaviours." A sequence of largely unconscious interpretation and adjustment creates our behaviour.

It is difficult for self-aware humans to realize that the environment is the driving force behind human interpretation, because introspection tells us that human behaviour is caused by human conscious intentions. In reality, it is meaningless to think of mind, body, and environment as existing separately. Our reality is composed of a complex of customs, social situations, personal experience, culture and objects, and our environment determines our being to an inconceivable extent. Awareness largely follows behaviour, rather than vice versa.

Some design practitioners have intuitively observed people in everyday life, examined these everyday interactions, and sublimated their thought from these observations into their design solutions (Suri 2005; Hosoe et al. 1991; Goto et al. 2004). They discover a lot about how people physically and perceptually blend with their surroundings. They look carefully at what people actually end up doing in everyday life: why have people put something here in a certain way? What are the people making a certain pose doing there and why do people respond to an object in the way they do? Why did people react in that way? Introspection can sometimes reveal what is of value to us behind these everyday interactions that occur around us all the time, but in fact we are not usually consciously aware of our actions and reactions. By this view, humans can be characterized as; *people who intuitively interpret what is of value for their purposes in their current environment and try to become harmonious with it in everyday life activities.*

To understand this phenomenon, there is a key concept – affordance – from ecological psychology. James J Gibson, in his book *The Ecological Approach to Visual Perception* (Gibson 1978), coined the term 'affordance' from the verb 'to afford'. According to his theory, a chair possesses an affordance for sitting, but the chair does not force a person into sitting. People may find themselves sitting without any awareness of having decided to sit. Further, a chair affords the prospect of sitting regardless of a person's health, condition or mood. Affordances seem to draw on our natural flow of action in specific situations. Every organism including humans utilizes affordances in the environment. Affordances are something that everyone knows intuitively and largely unconsciously; they are innumerable, complex and mysterious.

Similarly, people sometimes get healing from paintings, poems and music. They sometimes end up crying when they are in a church. They are then human, neither customer nor user. As Dutton suggests,

> the most recent research on universal features, for example in art, has come out of evolu-
> tionary psychology, which attempts to understand and explain the experience and capacities
> of the human mind in terms of characteristics it developed in the long evolutionary history
> of the human species. (Dutton 2001, p. 283)

Table 2.2 Categorization of audiences

Audience	Definition
Customer	A set of potential people based on segmentation variables such as demographic, geographic and psychographic criteria among others
User	People who have experience of use and generate knowledge with artefacts/products in a knowledge lifecycle
Person	People who intuitively interpret what is of value for their purposes in the current environment and seek balance in everyday activities
Human	People with the same evolutionary history and bodily structure and hence the same primitives for understanding information

In everyday life, we encounter the embodiment notion, resting on the idea that the mind and the body, or cognition and action, are fundamentally associated in human experience. Following a perspective based in the 'Experiential Realism' of (Lakoff 1987; Lakoff and Johnson 1999), we find that "human beings understand their experiences largely depending on basic, bodily interactions with physical environments, as well as on social and cultural interactions with other humans" (Waterworth et al. 2003, p. 137).

All human beings draw on the same primitive experiences that cover our shared embodied knowledge evolved over thousands, even millions of years (Waterworth et al. 2003; Hosoe 2006). Humans are organisms who share the same evolutionary history and hence, bodily structures and potential for experiences. Because of this, they also share the same primitives for understanding information – which is the fundamental principle underlying human-experiential design applied to interaction. The place of the human in a categorization of audiences is shown in Table 2.2.

The Virtual-Physical Dichotomy

Since the ubiquitous GUI was introduced and became the standard paradigm in HCI, it has contributed enormously to the development of society, especially the way we work. Recently, we have witnessed the emergence of a wider variety of HCI technologies, such as those implemented within sensor-based gaming environments, handheld smart phones with more intuitive onscreen interfaces and orientation sensors, etc., and these are now gradually penetrating society. However, we still cannot effectively utilize our skills for manipulating physical objects to any great extent, even though that would improve the nature of interaction. Research work on tangible interaction has been mostly focusing on numerous but narrow activities such as the manipulation of building blocks or shaping models out of virtual/physical clay (Ishii 2008).

Currently, we live in the physical world in which computers are distributed, with interaction windows onto the virtual world provided by the display, keyboard, and mouse, or touch-sensitive surface. It is not a surprising idea to combine in 'the interface' the virtual and the physical aspects of an interactive device, since the user sees the product itself as a unified physical/virtual system. But the rest of the physical world, and most of the bodily skills and experiences of the user, lie outside this unified and defined world. Users are further limited by a variety of factors, such as physical display constraints, input-output constraints, and social constraints. For example, physical display constraints mean that the user usually concentrates on only foreground tasks with full access to only a single display surface.

The evolution of interaction techniques has largely also been the history of improving the usability and appeal of the WIMP-based GUI. These work well in many situations, most obviously and importantly for many kinds of office or similar work. The work and the style of interaction have co-evolved and reinforced each other: we do the work we do because of the tools we have, and we have the tools we have because of the work we do.

Several researchers have discussed ways to modify or even escape from this self-perpetuating trend and have, for example, experimented with sensor-based techniques for interacting with virtual entities via the manipulation of physical objects in space (e.g. Ishii 2008; Ishii et al. 1998). Most of the broad range of new interfaces developed by HCI researchers are presented as alternatives to the current GUI paradigm and try, in one way or another, to diverge from the WIMP-based approach (Jacob et al. 2007). Better approaches for many types of people, including those with special needs such as the elderly and the socially or physically handicapped, draw on other principles such as free body movement, de-centralised displays, and tacit knowledge (Zacks et al. 2007; Schacter 1987; Benjamin et al. 1994).

We can find numerous emerging post-GUI/WIMP interaction styles, and they constitute a huge growing trend in the HCI literature, because of their clear advantages of bringing more real, more tangible and more usable interaction. Typical examples are; augmented reality, tangible interaction, ubiquitous and pervasive computing, context-aware computing, handheld, or mobile interaction and so on (Jacob et al. 2008). Recently, we have witnessed the emergence of a wider variety of HCI technologies, including handheld smart phones with more intuitive onscreen interfaces, which are pervasively penetrating into our everyday life.

Technology creates the virtual world, but also exists in the physical world with which the virtual often competes for our attention. Many of these new interaction styles clearly exhibit a combination of the physical and the virtual, sometimes called mixed reality. Today mixed realities of various kinds are an increasingly prevalent approach to interaction that strives to combine the physical and the virtual. Mixed reality is also a growing object of study for the HCI research community, as part of a widespread effort to develop viable and more flexible alternatives to WIMP-based GUIs. But do these interaction styles really have many benefits for those who use them? In terms of the perceptual and psychological aspects of use, the effect of these post-WIMP interaction styles has yet to be fully studied and understood.

Another post-WIMP trend is that digital media are becoming more pervasive in our built environments, and include devices such as video screens, electronic access systems, and sensor-based smart environments. But there is still a huge gap between the digital media and humans as bodies in physical space.

We predict that the intersection of sensory, cognitive and emotional aspects in emerging mixed realities will be significantly important in attempts to go a further step in the development of better combinations between the physical and virtual environment, in what we call *Blended Reality Space* (first proposed in Hoshi et al. 2009).

We return to the notion of blended reality space later in the book (especially in Chap. 5). In brief, it is an interactive mixed reality environment where the physical and the virtual are seamlessly combined and affect each other. In a true blending of the physical and the virtual, the technology itself would completely disappear from our perception. In such a situation, there will be no conscious effort of access to information (Waterworth and Waterworth 2010). It would then be possible to realize an ideal in which our activities are supported by technology and yet characterized by a natural flow of action, without any intrusion from the technology, from the physical-virtual divide. The human user would perceive and act directly, as in everyday life unmediated activities.

References

Alben L (1996) Quality of experience: defining the criteria for effective interaction design. Interactions 3(3):11–15

Bannon, L. (2011). Reimagining HCI: toward a more human-centered perspective. Interactions 18(4):50–57. NY, ACM

Battarbee K (2003) Defining co-experience. Paper presented at the the international conference on designing pleasurable products and interfaces. ACM Press, Pittsburgh

Benjamin LT, Hopkins JR, Nation JR (1994) Psychology, 3rd edn. Macmillan College Publishing Company, New York

Card SK, Moran TP, Newell A (1983) The psychology of human-computer interaction. Lawrence Erlbaum Associates, Mahwah

Colbert M (2005) User experience of communication before and during rendezvous: interim results. Pers Ubiquit Comput 9(3):134–141

Craik KJW (1943) The nature of explanation. Blackwell, London

Descartes R (1637) Discourse on the method, etc. Published on-line by Project Gutenburg. http://www.gutenberg.org/files/59/59-h/59-h.htm

Dourish P (2001) Where the action is: the foundation of embodied interaction. The MIT Press, Cambridge, MA

Dutton D (ed) (2001) Aaesthetic universals. Routledge, New York

Gibson JJ (1978) The ecological approach to visual perception. Lawrence Erlbaum Associates, Publishers, Hillsdale

Goto T, Sasaki M, Fukasawa N (2004) The ecological approach to design. Tokyo shoseki, Tokyo

Hassenzahl M (2008) User experience (UX): towards an experiential perspective on product quality. Paper presented at the IHM 2008. Metz, France

Hassenzahl M (2010) Experience design: technology for all the right reasons (synthesis lectures on human-centred informatics). Morgan and Claypool Publishers

Hassenzahl M, Tractinsky N (2006) User experience – a research agenda. Behav Inf Technol 25(2):90–97

Hekkert P (2006) Design aesthetics: principles of pleasure in design. Psychol Sci 48(2):157–172

Hevner AR, March ST, Park J, Ram S (2004) Design science in information systems research. MIS Quaterly 28(1):75–105

Hosoe I (2006) A trickster approach to interaction design. In: Bagnara S, Smith GC (eds) Theories and practice in interaction design. Lawrence Erlbaum Associates, Mahwah, pp 311–322

Hoshi K, Pesola UM, Waterworth EL, Waterworth J (2009) Tools, perspectives, and avatars in blended reality space. Cyberpsychology Behav 12(5):617–619

Hosoe I, Marinelli A, Sias R (1991) Play office: toward a new culture in the workplace. GC inc., Tokyo

Imaz M, Benyon D (2006) Desining with blends: conceptual foundations of human-computer interaction and software engineering. The MIT Press, Cambridge, MA

Ishii H (2008) Tangible bits: beyond pixels. Paper presented at the The 2nd International Conference on Tangible and Embedded Interaction. ACM Press, Kingston

Ishii H, Wisneski C, Brave S, Dahley A, Gorbet M, Ullmer B et al (1998) ambientROOM: integrating ambient media with architectural space. Paper presented at the CHI 98 conference summary on Human factors in computing systems, New York

ISO 13407 (1999) Human-centred design processes for interactive systems. International Organization for Standardization

Jacob RJK, Girouard A, Hirshfield LM, Horn MS, Shaer O, Solovey ET, et al (2007) Reality-based interaction: unifying the new generation of interaction styles paper presented at the CHI '07 extended abstracts on Human factors in computing systems

Jacob RJK, Girouard A, Hirshfield LM, Horn SM, Shaer O, Solovey ET et al (2008) Reality-Based interaction: a framework for Post-WIMP interface. Paper presented at the twenty-sixth annual SIGCHI conference on Human factors in computing systems, Florence, Italy

Johnson M (1987) The body in the mind: the bodily basis of meaning, imagination and reason. University of Chicago Press, Chicago

Keinonen T (2008) User-centred design and fundamental need paper presented at the The 5th Nordic conference on human-computer interaction

Lakoff G (1987) Woman, fire and dangerous things: what categories reveal about the mind. The University of Chicago Press, Chicago

Lakoff G, Johnson M (1980) Metaphors we live by Chicago. The University of Chicago Press, Chicago

Lakoff G, Johnson M (1999) Philosophy in the flesh: the embodied mind and its challenge to western thought. Basic Books, New York

Mactavish T (2009) The synthesis of design, technology, and business goals. In: Poggenpohl SH, Sato K (eds) Design integration: research and collaboration. Intellect Ltd, The University of Chicago Press, Chicago, pp 119–133

Mello S (2002) Customer-centric product definition. AMACOM, NewYork

Norman DA, Draper SW (1986) User centred system design: new perspective on human-computer interaction. Laurence Erlbaum Associates, Hillsdale

Oxford Dictionary of English (2003) Oxford University Press, Oxford

Reed ES (1996) Encountering the world: toward an ecological psychology. Oxford University Press, New York

Rosenzweig R (ed) (2003) Business frameworks. Fall 2003 course pack. Institute of Design, Illinois Institute of Technology, Chicago

Roto V, Law E, Vermeeren A, Hoonhout J (2011) User experience white paper: bringing clarity to the concept of experience. http://www.allaboutux.org/uxwhitepaper

Sato K (2009) Perspectives on design research. In: Poggenpohl S, Sato K (eds) Design integration: research and collaboration. Intellect Ltd, The University of Chicago Press, Chicago, pp 25–48

Schacter DL (1987) Implicit memory: history and current status. J Exp Psychol Learn Mem Cogn 13(3):501–518

Suchman L (2007) Human-machine reconfigurations. Cambridge University Press, New York

Suri JF (2005) Thoughtless acts?: observations on intuitive design. Chronicle books, San Francisco

Sward D, Macarthur G (2007) Making user experience a business strategy. Paper presented at the COST294-MAUSE affiliated workshop

Walls JG, Widmeyer GR, El Sawy OA (1992) Building an information system design theory for vigilant EIS. Inf Syst Res 3(1):36–58

Waterworth EL, Waterworth JA (2010) Mediated presence in the future. In: Bracken CC, Skalski PD (eds) Immersed in media: telepresence in everyday life. Routledge, Taylor & Francis Group, New York, pp 183–196

Waterworth JA, Lund A, Modjeska D (2003) Experiential design of shared information spaces. In: Höök K, Benyon D, Munro AJ (eds) Designing information spaces: the social navigation approach. Springer, Great Britain, pp 125–149

Waterworth JA, Ballesteros S, Peter C (2009a) User-sensitive home-based system for successful ageing paper presented at the 2nd international conference on Human System Interaction. Catania, pp. 542–545

Waterworth JA, Ballesteros S, Peter C, Bieber G, Kreiner A, Wiratanaya A, et al (2009b). Ageing in a networked society, social inclusion and mental stimulation. Paper presented at the 2nd International Conference on Pervasive Technologies Related to Assistive Environments

Zacks RT, Hasher L, Li KZH (2007) Human memory. In: Craik FIM, Salthouse TA (eds) The handbook of aging and cognition. LEA, Hillsdale, pp 293–358

Part II
Human-Experiential Design

In this Part, we outline our response to the problems of interaction in mixed reality and of design identified in Part I. *Human-experiential design* builds on the cognitive realist approach to understanding meaning of Lakoff and Johnson (1980) and others, as well as blending theory (e.g. Fauconnier and Turner 2003) and its application to software design (as proposed by Imaz and Benyon 2007). We then describe and explain how these views, combined with an understanding of the phenomena of mediated presence, can be used within design to help bridge the contextual reality gap that lies between different uses and users of everyday technological devices and systems.

Chapter 3
The Foundations of Human-Experiential Design

Abstract The main aim of this chapter is to set the scene for a new way of bridging the dichotomy between technological and human concerns. The *human-experiential design* approach offers a perspective from which both kinds of concern can be met, by providing a third way, which is neither objective nor subjective. It is a theoretical response to the design problems described in Chap. 2. The chapter presents the background to this alternative design practice and suggests that design can potentially play a part in integrating a range of attitudinal oppositions. It goes on to suggest how the designer's role should be re-positioned with respect to scientific design research.

Introduction

Our society has long been led by the development of scientific technology. Technology is the primary force behind the production and development of novel interactive systems and information/communication systems, and we live in what has been called the technology-driven society (Hara 2007). Much recent design in relation to the use of technology has been in service of what is essentially technological mastery, aiming to make good the promise of products and services in everyday life, and often whose forming activity was initiated by technology itself. A typical example is product design, which has largely become a presentation tool to introduce newly invented technology with attractive forms and interfaces.

All these newly designed products connect to the Internet, which itself contains attractive graphics designed for web sites and theatrical virtual realities discretely generated from numerical data. These design styles have sometimes penetrated into our physical environment and architecture, aiming to utilise and make attractive new materials and structures that technology also recently brought forth.

In contrast to the technology-driven approach, an experiential approach is the pursuit not of technology but of human sensual perception to invoke an animating force of design and creativity (Waterworth 1997, 2003). Experiential approaches to designing interactive systems have already been discussed in the HCI literature (e.g. Dourish 2001; Lund 2003; Fällman 2003; Imaz and Benyon 2006; Waterworth 1999).

© Springer International Publishing Switzerland 2016
J. Waterworth, K. Hoshi, *Human-Experiential Design of Presence in Everyday Blended Reality*, Human–Computer Interaction Series, DOI 10.1007/978-3-319-30334-5_3

In the rest of the present chapter, an alternative design practice – *human-experiential design* – is introduced as one that emphasizes the appropriate blending of technological and human concerns. It is neither purely technology-based nor purely experiential in the way this term is understood in HCI. Rather, it is attempts to explore a third way, which is neither purely objective nor subjective.

Design as Mediator

The human-experiential approach offers a way to understand the role of a blending process that can meaningfully bridge unbalanced dichotomies in the context of design. Although the importance of balance, blending and integration has already been discussed in other disciplines, there has been very little in terms of design. The development of design theory based on the logic of science has to try to demonstrate that science is capable of foreseeing design, even though it is still doubtful that there can ever be a truly rational methodology for design (Hosoe et al. 1991). Yet designers have the potential to play a key role in integrating opposites, and the present section discusses why they are suitable for the role.

The origin of modern design, whether taken as Ruskin and Morris or the Bauhaus, has always had a romantic tint from notions of idealistic social ethics. HCI, product designs, architecture, websites and so on all consist of technologies. Humans and technologies have, in a sense, co-evolved and technology, regarded as a product of science, has an ever more powerful influence on our society. In principle – and we believe in practice too – design can serve the role of integrating rationality and creative imagination starting from an idealistic social ethic that humans are central.

Humans are seen here not as separate from nature, as western cultural tradition would have it, but as an integrated part of nature and the built environment. Merleau-Ponty (1962, 2002) suggested that there are two sides to embodiment, bodies as physical structures and as lived, experiential structures, both biological and phenomenological, which are not opposed to each other but are continuously mutually engaged. In order to understand this profound notion of two sides enmeshed with each other, the practical embodiment of knowledge, cognition, and experience needs to be investigated in detail (Merleau-Ponty 1962, 2002). Merleau-Ponty's insight revealed a middle way - an *"entre-deux"* (Merleau-Ponty 1962, 2002) – between self and world, between the inner and the outer. The *entre-deux* can be understood as a space that comprises the gap between self and world, and allows for the continuity between them (Varela et al. 1993).

Historians, ethnologists, anthropologists and linguists have, from diverse sources, identified various champions to serve the role of unifying oppositions through their role as a mediator, and this can be seen as paralleling the role of the designer. For example Yamaguchi (2007), a cultural anthropologist, investigated mythological creatures and identified the role of 'trickster' as a catalyst that unifies two separate realities. Yamaguchi cites De Josselin de Jongh's book '*The Origin of the Divine Trickster*' (1929), which positioned the god Hermes-Mercury in the role of integrating all oppositions, beginning with that between man and woman, mature and immature, and internal and external. Yamaguchi also refers to Claude Levi-Strauss, who introduced a figure who plays the role of unifying of opposites in his writing, for example in *Les Mythologiques* (1964–1971).

A mythological character in Nigerian culture, called 'Hare', acts as the mediator between the king and the common people, between the city and the country, between astuteness and stupidity, between culture and nature (Yamaguchi 2007). In the works of Shakespeare, King Lear, the buffoon, was given the role of integrating rationality and irrationality, regality and madness, centre and periphery. In the twentieth century, new expressive forms and styles established by avant-garde artists such as Picasso were based on the image of Harlequin (Arlecchino) who was brought forth from Hermes-Mercury (Yamaguchi 2007; Hosoe et al. 1991). In Northern Europe, the Viking god 'Loki' played a role as mediator, between wisdom and misrule (Crossley-Holland 1982).

Hosoe et al. (1991) refers to the cultural role of the trickster as a dynamic catalyst and states that a "designer's role is to be a dynamic catalyst within the binomial center and outskirt" (p. 185). As Hosoe mentions in his book *Play Office* (1991), and as many other scholars have suggested, the catalyst or mediator has a vital role of communication that can ensure the balance of our world. Figures such as a trickster share the characteristics summarized below:

- They have a role as a mediator between separate aspects of the world.
- They never stay tranquil; they are continuously searching for something.
- They are intelligent but also take foolish actions ridiculed by the common people.
- Their behaviours are unpredictable and cannot be formalized.
- Their mischievous actions deconstruct pre-existent order and simultaneously produce new order.
- They destroy order and information. They promote entropy. Simultaneously they create a new structure in which entropy is transformed into negative-entropy.

Related to this reconciliation of opposites, Edward Hall (1969) introduced the terms low-context and high-context. Objective versus subjective can be partially replaced by low-context and high-context. According to Hall, in a high-context (HC) communication the information or message exchanged is either in the physical context or is embodied in the person (Fig. 3.1).

For example, a married couple that have been together for many years, or twins who have grown up together, can and do communicate through economic and

Fig. 3.1 High context-low context

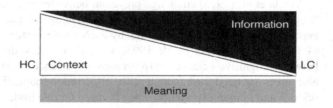

implicit ways of communication (HC), made possible by their sharing of context. In contrast, low-context (LC) communication can be found in information fixed in an explicit code, for example two lawyers communicating in a courtroom during a trial (Hall 1969). HC communication contains minimal information in the transmitted message itself, since the exchange is largely of pre-programmed information that is in the receiver and in the setting. Most of the information in LC communication, on the other hand, is in the transmitted message in order to compensate for a lack of shared context in the internal and external context (Hall 1969). High context communication underlies art, designs and products that are long-lived and slow to change. Low context communication changes more easily and rapidly and tends to be experienced as having less intrinsic value.

The imbalance between high and low context can be found in our everyday life with electronic and other tools. Consider how in the early days of mobile phones a few companies frequently brought out new models of their products. These mobile phones tended to be very low-context, and sometimes seemed to get out of date even before seeing the light of day. They frequently changed their functionality and sometimes their entire model of use, well before users had internalized the phone and its functionality into their experience.

Rapidly changing technologies, such as consumer electronics, restrict the possibilities for high contextual communication with users, and recent products have tended to settle on a more coherent style of interaction and use. Even when new features are added, companies such as Apple are very careful to maintain their overall look and feel, and the style of interaction seeks – with more or less success – to draw on bodily and other contextual factors, making them relatively high context compared to early versions of such products.

Some users have kept their early generation mobile phones for many years. They have become used to a certain design, and the communication between the user and the mobile phone has become internalized. This is another way in which high context communication has been developed. This works partly because new functionalities are excluded by the old design.

Acoustic musical instruments, for example the violin, have not changed the style of interaction or even their form over the last few centuries. Architecture styles adopted by many builders of churches in the West and temples in eastern cultures have been firmly established for hundreds of years, preserving religious beliefs and ideas up until today (Hall 1969). It can be said that high-contextuality places great importance on the need for being fixed and stable, while low-contextuality does the opposite. We need a development strategy for balancing two apparently contradictory needs, one which design could and should pursue.

Varela et al. (1993) challenge prevalent belief throughout cognitive science that "cognition consists of the representation of a world that is independent of our perceptual and cognitive capacities by a cognitive system that exists independent of the world" (Varela et al. 1993, xx). They stress the separation that exists between cognitive science and everyday experience of our present world. They also stress the need for having a sense of common foundation integrating cognitive science and human experience. They focused on one tradition that derives from the eastern philosophy of examining experience, what the eastern philosophers called *mindfulness,* which refers to awareness of being in the here and now. Their – at the time – unique aim was to build a bridge that links eastern philosophy and the western tradition of science, spanning human experience and cognitive science, by applying the concept of *non-self* and *non-dualism* that grew out of *mindfulness.*

In the domain of neuroscience, it is well known that there are functional asymmetries between the human cerebral cortices. Meinard Simon Du Pui suggested as far back as 1780 that mankind has a double brain with a double mind, what he called *Homo Duplex* (Taylor 2008). In his 1981 Nobel lecture Roger Sperry commented:

> ... The same individual can be observed to employ consistently one or the other of two distinct forms of mental approach and strategy, much like two different people, depending on whether the left or right hemisphere is in use. (http://nobelprize.org, 1981)

The neuroscientist Jill Bolte Taylor (2008), writing about her own experience of having a stroke, emphasises the importance of shifting from unbalanced brain functions towards a more correct balance. She describes the left- and right-brain functions with the terms doing-consciousness and being-consciousness. According to her, the left-brain can be characterized as the doing-consciousness that is trained to perceive oneself as a solid thing, separate from others, while the right brain presides over the being-consciousness that perceives the whole and relishes a natural state of flowing. In western society, the left-brain has often reigned as the seat of our consciousness through linguistic, sequential, methodological, rational, and intellectual activity. But if we stay unilaterally in the left-brain, our thinking ends up being predominantly analytic and critical, rigid and lacking flexibility.

On the other hand, to the right brain, only the present moment exists by this account, and each moment is vigorous and animated with sensation. That is the moment of the now, timeless and eternal. Rules and regulations do not exist; the right brain has no ability for judging the correct or wrong way of doing something. Our right brain takes things as they are without inhibition or judgment. The exploration of the possibilities that each present moment brings is intuitive and creative. The right brain is spontaneous, carefree, and imaginative. It allows our artistic being to flow freely. The right brain, if it is dominant, gives a sense of wholeness without a self who exists as a single, solid entity separate from everything else. The right brain has an ability to perceive how everything is related, connected and shared, and how every single thing unifies as one to form the whole. The right-brain function reminds us of the characteristics of the trickster, which are amusement, ludicrousness, omnipresence, entropy, freewheeling and so on.

Along with many other commentators, Taylor (2008) consistently stresses the need for creating a healthy balance between these two characters, which "enables us the ability to remain cognitively flexible enough to welcome change (right hemisphere), and yet remain concrete enough to stay a path (left hemisphere)" (p. 138).

The concept of mediator/facilitator is nothing new in interaction design. In the domains of HCI, CSCW, and related contextual research such as ethnography and participatory design, the importance of mediator or facilitator has long been discussed (Schuler and Namioka 1993; Nardi 1993; Wiberg 2001). The social scientist or applied ethnographer has been viewed as an interface between a user and a designer. The researcher collects primary information or uses secondary information to get insight about user needs. The researcher translates the information and proposes a document as a way of expressing design criteria. The designer then translates these criteria into concept sketches, scenarios, or early prototypes. The translations may or may not be used during the process for usability testing.

Participatory design gives a shared workshop space for a team of people who represent the stakeholders, such as users, designers, marketers, management people and developers, to understand needs and preferences in the development process. The results are formulated as design criteria that reflect user requirements and business goals. Lists of subjects, problems, issues, and questions are introduced through which the facilitator conducts the workshop. The facilitator induces discussion and helps communication among all the stakeholders, ensuring that both planned and unplanned issues are covered (Kaner et al. 2007).

In all these cases, the mediator is an essential part of the design process. Design, as an activity, works through the mediator. The mediator in human-experiential design has an essential role in seeking the design aspect of reality, in essence responding to the question of what it means to be human. We will now explore 'design' as represented in ordinary design science and research and bring certain key issues into the open.

Issues in Design Science and Research

We have discussed oppositions in our view of reality, such as the subjective-objective dichotomy, and introduced the designer's role as a dynamic catalyst that can integrate opposing elements. Here, we investigate how the designer's role can be positioned with respect to scientific design research. An alternative framework, which is neither objective nor subjective, a more integrated blend in Design Science, is proposed. But without first making clear what we see as the different types of design research, our described understanding of design science will be confusing, since there are a variety of perspectives on design research.

Design Knowledge in Design Practice

According to Sato (2009, p. 27), two types of design research can be identified.

1. The practice of developing information for a particular design project that includes a number of activities for gathering information such as customer/user needs, social issues, markets, competitive products, and related technologies. This design research focuses on understanding customers' and users' needs for developing artefacts/products from the user's point of view. This is generally called user-centred design research.

2. The practice of developing a general formalization of knowledge that includes theories, methods, principles, and tools that can be applicable as resources for the knowledge development cycle. The generated knowledge is shared across different design practices and commonly verifiable from an academic point of view. This is further divided into two distinct areas of interest, general design research and domain-specific design research (Sato, p. 28).

- General design research is the scientific study of the acts of design, which leads to general design theories and methodologies that provide general models of design process and knowledge, and contributes to improvements in the practice of design.
- Domain-specific design research is the study of the subjects of design, which leads to the development of knowledge about specific domains of design concern. HCI, for example, is one of the domains of design concern.

This categorization of design research is summarized in Table 3.1. General design research is composed of a variety of design theories and methodologies, which are categorized as descriptive or prescriptive. General design research has been identified with two aspects of design research, design theory and design methodology (Tomiyama 2009). According to Tomiyama (2009), design theory focuses on scientific study relevant to a number of such design activities as "design process, design activities, design knowledge, and designed artefacts/products" (p. 49), which contribute to further development of design theories and methodologies. On the other hand, design methodology is applied in design practice, for effectively supporting design and process, which is aimed at better design results.

Table 3.1 Categorization of design research

Design research	Research type	Aspect of research	Knowledge	Domains
(1) The practice of developing information for a particular design project	(e.g.) User research Market research	Information development	(e.g.) Statistical data Contextual information Experimental data	
(2) The practice of developing a conceptualized body of knowledge	(2a) General design research	General theory/method development	(e.g.) Descriptive models Prescriptive models	(e.g.) Human-computer interaction Information systems
	(2b) Domain-specific design research	Design theory/method development	Design methods, frameworks and principles	Design (sustainable healthcare, etc.)

Tomiyama (2009) pointed out that "scientific understanding helps researchers to identify what to research, and helps design practitioners to correctly understand what can be done and what cannot with a particular type of design methodology" (p. 50).

Table 3.1 suggests that 'design knowledge' could be externalized and could be a matter of the intellect, but can 'design' be conceptually explained through language? As far as 'design' addresses all the natural dimensions of our experiences, including our sensual perception, it is not easy to externalize. So 'design' is not merely a matter of language, nor just a matter of the intellect. Here, a question arises: What is scientific knowledge in design research actually?

Jurgen Habermas (1998, 33) discussed a distinction between know-how and know-that. A person with habituated skills has 'know-how' which is the understanding in which a skilled practitioner crafts or executes something. On the other hand, 'know-that' is the explicit forms of knowledge in which a person is able to know-how. A number of design activities can be seen as 'know-how' based, originating from a craft-work perspective and therefore difficult to express in the explicit forms of language, and thus not adequately covered by today's fast evolving and complicated design process accounts (Poggenpohl 2009; Krippendorff 1995; Owen 1998; Buchanan 2001).

Humans have both embodied and abstract forms of knowledge. They affect each other, and are not easily dissociable. In scientific research, researchers and scholars mainly deal with descriptive knowledge with an explicit form of language. On the other hand, humans also have unexpressed knowledge, so-called tacit or implicit knowledge (Polanyi 1966). In general, implicit knowledge can be communicated by shared meaning between people.

Effective engagement between explicit and implicit knowledge could in principle enhance creativity in the design process and open up a new research area in design disciplines. Practitioners in business and design management have tried to adopt the term tacit knowledge to describe inexpressible mechanisms of individual and organizational creativity. However, the approach has not been successful (Nonaka 1991). One reason is that there is a lack of understanding of the notion of creativity. Ironically, creativity itself is hard to illustrate and externalize. If the context of design activity is preceded with inexpressible knowledge, creativity is also equal to, or part of, tacit knowledge.

In reality, designer practitioners generally ignore the results of design research on the assumption that design research is inapplicable and useless to design practice. Hence, designers execute their own design process without explicitly using theories and methodologies. Designers will claim that design solutions that come from scientific theories and methods are relatively frail compared with design solutions obtained on the basis of intuition (Tomiyama 2009). In other words, even though design can be improved by scientific studies addressing, for example, accessibility, usability, or acceptability, it is not considered by designers to be suitable for aesthetic and sensitive design in practice.

Certainly, there is something not easy to externalize in design knowledge (and not only design knowledge but also human knowledge in general). But, designers clearly have an understanding of what 'design' is and do design based on their understanding. If not, they could not externalize their idea and could not apply the externalization in developing artefacts/products. It should be possible to identify scientific knowledge in design research, in which rationality and creativity are integrated, if human creativity is revealed through investigating the process of understanding.

Next, we look at design knowledge from a problem-solving paradigm. This reveals dichotomies, gaps and lacks that must be integrated effectively to develop IT artefacts. The investigation also helps identify how scientific knowledge of design research can be positioned from the human-experiential design perspective.

Design Knowledge in a Problem-Solving Paradigm

The needed unification of apparent opposites has become an increasingly obvious issue within the information systems (IS) discipline, in efforts to produce effective health information systems (Walls et al. 1992; March and Smith 1995). These kinds of issue have also long been discussed in information systems (IS) design (Boland et al. 1994; Glass 1999; Winograd 1996, 1997; Lyytinen and Hirschheim 1988). We can find several dichotomies in different aspects of this work, dealing with people, organization, technology, and design. For example, many IS researchers and practitioners have discussed distinct paradigms of behavioural science and design science, which are foundational to the IS discipline (Walls et al. 1992; Hevner et al. 2004).

Whereas the behavioural science paradigm has its roots in natural or physical science research methods that explore what is true (i.e., principles and laws), the design science paradigm has its roots in engineering and the sciences of the artificial, which seek to create what is effective (Simon 1996; Tsichritzis 1997; Denning 1997; Hevner et al. 2004). Alexander (1969) commented that "scientists try to identify the components of existing structures, designers try to shape the components of structure". Fielden (1975) described engineering design as "the use of scientific principles, technical information and imagination in the definition of a structure, machine or system to perform pre-specified functions with the maximum economy and efficiency". Discussions of Alexander (1969) and Fielden (1975) are about the static structure of architectures and engineering, but can be applied to the dynamic structure of information systems as well (Walls et al. 1992).

Design knowledge in IS research has been developed within the interaction between business strategy, IT strategy, organizational infrastructure, and IS infrastructure (Hevner et al. 2004). In order to develop and implement information systems effectively within the interaction between them, problems need to be understood and successfully solved. Design knowledge and theory in IS disciplines has been defined as "a prescriptive theory that integrates normative and descriptive theories into design paths intended to produce more effective information systems" (Walls et al. 1992). According to Silver and Markus (1995), one reason is that

"Information systems are implemented within an organization for the purpose of improving the effectiveness and efficiency of that organization". Concrete prescriptions have been defined as constructs (vocabulary and symbols), models (abstractions and representations), methods (algorithms and practices), and instanti-ations (implemented and prototype systems) (Hevner et al. 2004; March and Smith 1995).

The objective of systems theory is to identify properties common to all types of system and to use these properties to understand and describe specific systems (Walls et al. 1992). Methods of effective development and a type of instantiation for a particular class of models (Markus et al. 2002) are then prescribed. Constructs help to communicate between problems defined and solutions represented (Schön 1983). Models use constructs to conceptualize a real world phenomenon, and visualize the design problem and its solution space (Simon 1996). Models are also used to understand problems and solution, and to represent the effects of decision-makings and changes in the real situation in which problem and solution components are engaged (Hevner et al. 2004). Methods define processes, which guide how to find a solution space. Constructs, models, and methods need to be integrated effectively to implement solutions in a system in real situations. Instantiations, in other words, designing and prototyping, demonstrate feasibility, enabling the evaluation of an artefact's suitability for its intended purpose (Hevner et al. 2004; March and Smith 1995).

Design knowledge in user-centred design, including not only systems design but also product and interaction design more broadly and industrial design in general, has two aspects, a product (artefact) and a process (set of activities) (Hevner et al. 2004; Walls et al. 1992). As defined previously, a user-centred design process can be seen as a process centring on the knowledge lifecycle that includes knowledge of use, knowledge of design and the user who generates knowledge through interpretation of embedded design knowledge in artefacts/products. The goal of developing knowledge continuously shifts between design processes and designed artefacts. The design process is thus a knowledge development cycle that generates innovative products/artefacts. Evaluation of both the artefacts and the process is needed in order to understand the problems for which the process of knowledge cycle is effectively carried out, which in turn improve both the quality of the product/artefact and the design process. Knowledge development is a lifecycle loop repeatedly conducted until the final artefact is designed (Markus et al. 2002).

Methods for developing knowledge in design research and in IS research share a paradigm in which they pursue the same goal, which is a problem solving. The developed theories prescribe effectiveness of system solutions for a particular class of user requirement (Markus et al. 2002, p. 180). Design knowledge in these domains focuses on situated utility (March and Smith 1995). As the categorization of audiences shown previously (see Fig. 3.2) reveals, the process of understanding on a more human scale, more experientially and aesthetical sensitive is not discussed or investigated.

Fig. 3.2 Humans in everyday life and rational scientific design research

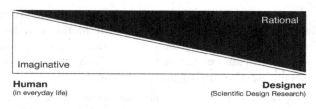

Rational

Imaginative

Human
(in everyday life)

Designer
(Scientific Design Research)

Theoretical Models

Design exists alongside both absolute objectivity and purely subjective intuition, in other words, rationality and imagination. Although it contains implicit notions not easy to externalize in words, only externalized expressions are conceptualized as theoretical models in science. It seems, therefore, that design is hardly accepted as science. But what is a conceptual model? What is a theoretical model?

Many different models exist, in settings from everyday life to advanced science. For example, teachers have a model answer to an exam question. Parents should be role models for children. Mechanical models explain how a machine works, and can be used for generating and analysing data from experiments models, such as those using scale models of vehicles in wind tunnels. There is a model (a mould) to reproduce machines or plastic artefacts. Linguists investigate grammars and writing systems and explain them with models of language. Cultural anthropologists use theoretical models rooted in culture. Highly abstract forms of models are often used to explain entire cultures that are themselves a series of contextual models for behaviour and thought (Hall 1969). Mathematical models are used to express scientifically reliable qualities, quantities, and relationships encountered in life, predominantly by natural scientists.

We can find different types of models used to explain cognitive systems, in science, philosophical systems and even in myths (Hall 1969). Scientists study only those things that can be externalized as models. They use models in order to experiment with how things work, and try to foresee how things would function in the future. They judge the effectiveness of a model by exploring how consistent it is, not as an everyday life concern but as a mechanical or philosophical system.

In the design domain (called 'scientific design'), theoretical models are usually composed of theory, method and tool. Theory is a generalized and abstract form of explanation, which helps to understand the salient issues that we try to design for or around. It helps also to describe particular phenomena, but describing is not the same as designing. As pointed out earlier in the example of designing a chair, we can describe what a chair is in a generalized way, but it is not easy to design a satisfactory chair. Method in many forms of physical and digital design is a tool of understanding actions relevant to a domain of problem. The generalization of theory, the development and testing of method, and the creation of a tool are explicit activities based on critical analysis and experimenting until a solution is found (Poggenpohl 2009).

Sometimes designers and design researchers blindly accept that methods guarantee a satisfactory design achievement. Methods are however not a guarantee of superior design. We should not forget that a design method is a tool in the explicit way, and it can be said that all theorizing processes and theoretical models are incomplete. Hall (1976) pointed out that:

> by definition, they are abstractions and therefore leave things out. What things they leave out is as important as, if not more important than, what they do not, because it is what is left out that gives structure and form to the system. (Hall 1976, p. 14)

This 'leaving out' has tended to equal avoidance of the complicatedness of the real world and of humans. Design has been 'scientific' to the extent that it has kept away from dealing with everyday concerns. But beneath the clearly perceived, highly explicit surface phenomena there lies the rest of the world. The underneath and the surface are inseparable.

Integrated Design Science: Towards Human-Experiential Design

An integrated approach to design seeks to take account of both overt and covert aspects, the implicit and the explicit, the things that are externalised in talk and the things that are not. In this book we propose human-experiential design as such an approach that can be applied to our everyday lives, including aspects that are implicit, often unconscious, and are not easily externalisable in words – ways which, as it were, only our bodies know.

Information and communication technologies already, and will increasingly, mediate our experience of the world and people around us, from mobile phones to home entertainment and immersive computer games, to living/housing environment, public spaces architecture in general (Wiberg 2011). As we discussed in Chap. 1, the future of the human sense of presence, of being in the world in the here and now, will reflect the rapid development of ever more pervasively penetrating digital technologies (Waterworth et al. 2010). The ultimate in presence is a perceived experience through technology as if directly though the human senses and perceptual processes – the illusion of non-mediation (Lombard and Ditton 1997).

It is currently unusual to achieve this state, since technology is most often designed on the basis of explicit conceptual knowledge, while human sensation and perception is rather an embodied implicit phenomenon. Human beings therefore have to adapt to the mediating technologies, even though human behaviours are naturally expressed as a natural flow of action based on the experience of being present in an environment. How can technology be designed to allow humans to experience an integrated sense of presence in the physical world as mediated by technology? In user-centred HCI, we usually answer the question of how to design in this way: "Designers should conduct user studies, users should be involved in a design process." But is this enough?

People still struggle to understand and use computers, mobile phones and other embedded computing devices, whose designs are largely based on the formalization of human cognition of the world, and which break the human sense of presence potentially invoked in computer-mediated environments.

Although design research for the most part has been evolving in order to bridge the gap between designer and user, mutual understanding can be especially difficult to share across different cultures, knowledge, values, and assumptions. It can be said that the problem of the gap in mutual understanding between designers and users may come from a blind acceptance of objectivism based on the prestige of science.

The gap between designer and user can thus be seen as the gap between objectivism (the rational) and subjectivism (the imagination) as shown in Fig. 3.2. Up until now, scientific design research has tried to establish an independent position through intellectualizing and with a disregard for the nonverbal. By its nature, it is not easy for designers to explain their own irrationality or that of users. Although irrationality does not yield to logic, it is an intrinsic part of life. We can experientially understand that we are not always living by logical reasoning. The irrational comprises a significant portion of our everyday life behaviour. It is time for design researchers and designers to resign themselves to that fact. Instead of rejecting irrationality in designers and users, we should take a healthier attitude and seek to integrate the irrational and rational.

Designers in scientific design research and users live in different cultures. Understanding each other, each culture and the world and explicating the irrational are inseparable aspects of the same process. As Hall (1969) pointed out: "Culturally-based paradigms place obstacles in the path to understanding" (p. 220). Misunderstandings between designer and user are not unfamiliar. In verbal communication in everyday life, people need a flexible adaptability in worldview, as well as expertise in finding the appropriate metaphor to communicate the relevant parts of a limited sharing of experiences. They must emphasize the shared experiences while toning others down, and metaphor draws on what is shared. Metaphorical imagination is a critical skill for designers to creating harmony through communicating a shared experience with users.

The human-experiential approach to design is aimed at integrating creative imagination and rationality. To understand what cannot be comprehended totally, for example senses, feelings and aesthetic experiences, involves seeing one kind of thing in terms of another. This is the integration of reason and imagination, which can be described as metaphorical thought (Lakoff and Johnson 1980). According to Lakoff and Johnson (1980) "our conceptual system is metaphorical in nature. The essence of metaphor is understanding and experiencing one kind of thing in terms of another" (p. 5). Metaphors are rooted in physical and cultural experience. A metaphor can serve as a vehicle for understanding a concept only by virtue of its experiential basis.

Designers use metaphors in graphic design, interface design and interaction design, and so on. Metaphors work effectively in relations perceived in similar ways between the designer and the user. If the user doesn't have the same cultural background as the designer, it is difficult to understand them. Even in the same or similar cultures, there can be significant misunderstandings. But if an artefact is understood, meaning is shared between the designer and the user. When they share it, the reality gap between the designer and the user is bridged. They understand aspects of the meaning of the artefact and of its functionality as well.

This perceived understanding may involve all the natural dimensions of our experiences, including sense experiences such as colour, shape, texture, and sound. Metaphors, integrating imagination and rationality, are as much as a part of our functioning as our sensory perception, and as precious. Designer and user share the meaning (the sense) as though the ability to comprehend through metaphor is like seeing, touching or hearing the same thing. Metaphor is not merely a matter of language, just as design is not merely a matter of the intellect. Experience through the designed object is as if they share the same embodiment for understanding information.

It is not too much to say again and again that designers should have the ability to put themselves in the users' place, to 'sense' their 'sense', to be in their situation, to see through their eyes. The core principle underlying shared feeling, or empathy, is that designer and user are connected when they are both conscious of their *here and now*. This is how the sharing of primitives for understanding works. In their design activities, designers should be conscious of the present. Users perceive consciously in the present (and only in the present) through using the designed object. We return to the importance of the here and now in Part III.

Human-experiential design takes on a different point of view from one based only on designers' tacit knowledge. Rather, it focuses on the reality of human beings having the same primitives of experience. While it may be that much evolutionary memory is conserved in our senses, much memory is, we believe, hidden for future survival, or transformed to adapt to the present time. If we are patient, these memories will emerge to be appreciated someday (Hosoe 2006). Human-experiential design seeks to play a modest role in redressing unbalanced dichotomies and move towards increasing balance. A human-experiential designer acts as a mediator for blending apparently contradictory viewpoints. In the next chapter (Chap. 4) we start to explain how this is done.

References

Alexander C (1969) Notes on the synthesis of form. Harvard University, Boston

Boland RJ, Tenkasi RV, Te'eni D (1994) Designing information technology to support distributed cognition. Organ Sci 5(3):456–475

Buchanan R (2001) Design research and the new learning. Des Issues 17(4):3–23

Crossley-Holland K (1982) The Penguin Book of Norse myths: Gods of the Vikings. Penguin Books, London

De Josselin de Jong JPB (1929) De oorsprong van den goddelijken bedrieger (The origin of the divine trickster). Mededeelingen der Koninklijke Akademie van Wetenschappen. Amsterdam: Koninklijke Akademie van Wetenschappen. Afdeeling Letterkunde, pp 1–29. Deel 68, Serie B

Denning PJ (1997) A new social contract for research. Commun ACM 40(2):132–134

Dourish P (2001) Where the action is: the foundation of embodied interaction. The MIT Press, Cambridge, MA

Fällman D (2003) In romance with the materials of mobile interaction. Umeå University, Umeå

Fielden GBR (1975) Engineering design. British Standards Institution, London

Glass RL (1999) On design. IEEE Softw 16(2):103–104

Habermas J (1998) On the pragmatics of communication. MIT Press, Cambridge, MA

Hall ET (1969) The hidden dimension. Anchor, Doubleday, Garden City

Hara K (2007) Designing design. Lars Muller Publishers, Baden

Hevner AR, March ST, Park J, Ram S (2004) Design science in information systems research. MIS Q 28(1):75–105

Hosoe I (2006) A trickster approach to interaction design. In: Bagnara S, Smith GC (eds) Theories and practice in interaction design. Lawrence Erlbaum Associates, Mahwah, pp 311–322

Hosoe I, Sias R, Marinelli A (1991) Play office: toward a new culture in the workplace. GC Inc, Tokyo

Imaz M, Benyon D (2006) Desining with blends: conceptual foundations of human-computer interaction and software engineering. The MIT Press, Cambridge, MA

Kaner S, Lind L, Toldi C, Fisk S, Berger D (2007) Facilitator's guide to participatory decision making. Jossey-Bass, San Franscisco

Krippendorff K (1995) Redesigning design; an invitation to a responsible future. In: Tahkokallio P, Vihma S (eds) Design: pleasure or responsibility. University of Art and Design, Helsinki, pp 138–162

Lakoff G, Johnson M (1980) Metaphors we live by Chicago. The University of Chicago Press, Chicago

Levi-Strauss C (1964–1971) Mythologiques I–IV (trans. Weightman J, Weightman D 1969–1981). University of Chicago Press, Chicago

Lombard M, Ditton T (1997) At the heart of it all: the concept of presence. J Comput Mediated-Commun. http://onlinelibrary.wiley.com/doi/10.1111/j.1083-6101.1997.tb00072.x/abstract

Lund A (2003) Massification of the intangible: a investigation into embodied meaning and information visualization. Umeå University, Umeå

Lyytinen K, Hirschheim R (1988) Informations systems as rationale discourse: an application of Habermas theory of communicative action Scandinavian. J Manag 4(1,2):19–30

March ST, Smith GF (1995) Design and natural science research on information technology [Amsterdam: Elsevier Science Publishers B.V.]. Decis Support Syst 15(4):251–266

Markus ML, Majchrzak A, Gasser L (2002) Design theory for systems that support emergent knowledge process. MIS Q 26(3):1979–1212

Merleau-Ponty M (1962, 2002) Phenomenology of perception. Routledge, London

Nardi BA (1993) A small matter of programming: perspectives on end user computing. The MIT Press, Cambridge, MA

Nonaka I (1991) The knowledge-creating company. Harv Bus Rev 6:96

Owen C (1998) Design research: building the knowledge base. Des Stud 19(1):9–20

Poggenpohl S (2009) Time for change: building a design discipline. In: Poggenpohl S, Sato K (eds) Design integration: research and collaboration. Intellect Ltd, The University of Chicago Press, Chicago, pp 3–24

Polanyi M (1966) The tacit dimension. The University of Chicago Press, Chicago

Sato K (2009) Perspectives on design research. In: Poggenpohl S, Sato K (eds) Design integration: research and collaboration. Intellect Ltd, The University of Chicago Press, Chicago, pp 25–48

Schön D (1983) The reflective practitioner: how professionals think in action. Basic Books, New York

Schuler D, Namioka A (1993) Participatory design: principles and practices. CRC Press, Boca Raton

Silver M, Markus L (1995) The interaction technology interactive model. MIS Quarterly 19:360–390

Simon H (1996) The sciences of the artificial, 3rd edn. MIT Press, Cambridge, MA

Taylor JB (2008) My stroke of insight. Hodder & Stoughton Ltd., London

Tomiyama T (2009) Design theory and methodology for engineering design practices. In: Poggenpohl S, Sato K (eds) Design integration: research and collaboration. Intellect Ltd, The University of Chicago Press, Chicago

Tsichritzis D (1997) The design of interaction. In: Denning P, Metcalfe R (eds) Beyond calculation: the next 50 years of computing. Springer, New York, pp 259–265

Varela FJ, Thompson E, Rosch E (1993) The embodied mind: cognitive science and human experience. MIT Press, Cambridge, MA

Walls JG, Widmeyer GR, El Sawy OA (1992) Building an information systems design theory for vigilant EIS. Inf Syst Res 3(1):36–59

Waterworth JA (1997) Creativity and sensation: the case for synaesthetic media. Leonardo 30(4):327–330

Waterworth JA (1999) Spaces, places, landscapes, and views: experiential design of Shred information spaces. In: Munro AJ, Hook K, Benyon D (eds) Social navigation of information space. Springer, London

Waterworth JA (2003) Virtual realisation: supporting creative outcomes in medicine and music. Psychology 1(4):410–427

Waterworth JA, Waterworth EL, Mantovani F, Riva G (2010) On feeling (the) present. J Conscious Stud 17(1–2):167–188

Wiberg C (2001) Bridging the gap between designers and ethnographers by using a facilitator. In: Glimelli H, Juhlin O (eds) The social production of technology with things. BAS Publishers, Gothenburg

Wiberg M (2011) Interactive textures for architecture and landscaping. Digital elements and technologies. IGI Global, Hershey

Winograd T (1996) Bringing design to software. ACM, New York

Winograd T (1997) The design of interaction. In: Denning P, Metcalfe R (eds) Beyond calculation: the next 50 years of computing. Springer, New York, pp 149–162

Yamaguchi M (2007) Connecting whales and humans: contemporary development of small coastal whaling activity in Japan and the role of gunners (in Japanese). Ecosophia 19:86–105

Chapter 4
Designing with Blends

Abstract This chapter describes the conceptual grounding of blending as a design process, giving the potential for the creation of blended reality spaces as interactive environments where the physical and the virtual are seamlessly combined. The link between blends and the human-experiential approach to interaction design is then presented and discussed, using a standard figurative representation of the blending process. This helps us to understand the role of blending in creating a meaningful bridge between the otherwise unbalanced processes of cognition and action in mixes of the physical and the virtual. The importance of balance as appropriate blending in the development of better interactive systems for a range of application areas is stressed.

Introduction: Combining the Physical and the Virtual

Technology creates the virtual world, but itself exists in the physical world – with which the virtual often competes for our attention. Many new interaction styles strongly emphasise a combination of the physical and the virtual, sometimes called mixed reality (Jacob et al. 2007; Chalmers and Maccoll 2003; Rogers et al. 2002). Today, mixed realities of different kinds represent an increasingly prevalent approach to designing interactive experiences. Mixed reality is also a growing object of study for the HCI research community, as part of a widespread effort to develop viable and more flexible alternatives to WIMP-based GUIs. Many of the broad range of new interfaces developed by HCI researchers are seen as alternatives to the current GUI paradigm and try, in one way or another, to diverge from the WIMP-based approach (Jacob et al. 2008). For example, sensor-based techniques for interacting with virtual entities via the manipulation of physical objects in space have been explored by several researchers (see Ishii 2008).

We have also witnessed the emergence of a wider variety of HCI technologies in products during the last few years, such as those implemented in physical environments equipped with sensors, or in handheld smart phones with more intuitive onscreen interfaces and inbuilt orientation sensors. These and other recent innovations are now gradually penetrating society, and emerge as a growing trend in the HCI literature. Representative examples fall under the headings of augmented

© Springer International Publishing Switzerland 2016

J. Waterworth, K. Hoshi, *Human-Experiential Design of Presence in Everyday Blended Reality*, Human–Computer Interaction Series, DOI 10.1007/978-3-319-30334-5_4

reality, tangible interaction, ubiquitous and pervasive computing, context-aware computing, handheld, or mobile interaction and so on (Jacob et al. 2008). But there is still a huge gap between these interactive media and our selves as bodies in physical space. We need a clear understanding of the scope of this phenomenon, especially its perceptual and psychological aspects.

The history of HCI can in fact be seen as largely that of the evolution of the standard WIMP interface composed of desktop metaphors. When metaphors don't work well, they lead to people to develop inappropriate expectations of technologies (Imaz and Benyon 2006). And yet we have been slow in finding replacements for the uniquely successful metaphor of the desktop. To move beyond this and other existing metaphors, we need to consider how they are actually used, more as blends than as analogies with other things. In order to understand how blends are framed and formed, we need to get a picture of metaphors and how metaphors and blends actually work together. This will also help us to understand the embodiment notion, derived from our bodily and social experiences, and how it may be used in HCI design.

Metaphors and Design

Metaphors have been used in the design of digital devices for many years, though their use has been far from uncontroversial (e.g. Nelson 1999). The well recognized personal computer user interfaces have been at least partially designed on this basis – the 'desktop metaphor'. The idea was that the designer of a desktop interface explicitly tries to draw on people's knowledge of office work to help them understand the operation of the computer they are using. So metaphor is the well-known approach to the design of HCI, one which draws on users' experience in a different domain to assist their understanding of the computer system (Waterworth et al. 2003). Users appreciate such metaphors when their previous experiences are suitable for comprehending some new interaction, but will criticize metaphorical designs when they don't understand them or what they are for (Imaz and Benyon 2006).

Over the past 20 years, more and more computer interfaces have adopted a design style ostensibly based on this metaphor, and this has spread to other devices such as mobile phones, digital cameras, audio-visual equipment, and to some extent web sites. The metaphors will work well when the designer and the user perceive them in similar ways. But while metaphors are provided to let people bring their previous experiences to understand new interactions, they often lead to people developing different understandings of the purpose of some features, even within the same cultural environment. Much of this confusion arises because metaphor is not well understood by designers. That means that the embodied aspects of metaphor, which are derived from our bodily, social and cultural experience, are not well used. Next we consider why this might be the case.

In order to gain insight into how metaphors work in different cultures, Lakoff and Johnson (1980) give the example of cultures where arguments are viewed in terms of war.

Argument Is War

According to Lakoff and Johnson (1980), people in a culture that instantiates this metaphor understand, feel and act in argument as if physically in battle. In the culture, arguments are partially structured by the concept of war, such as attack, defend, shoot down, etc. This is a linguistic battle, of course, but the meaning is projected from the physical experience of battle. If, in contrast, there exists a culture where arguments are viewed in terms of dance, they will have a discourse structured in terms of various aspects of dancing. We can assume that people in this culture similarly understand and experience *argument* in terms of *dance performance*. They live in a culture where in arguing no one wins or loses, and no one is attacking or defending.

Our (human) thought processes are made up of metaphors in most part, and we act according to the way we imagine things, which can vary from culture to culture because metaphors are rooted in physical and cultural experiences (Lakoff and Johnson 1980). They can also vary within a culture, because no culture is entirely homogenous. Michel Polanyi (1966) has pointed out that "our message had left something behind that we could not tell, and its reception must rely on it that the person addressed will discover that which we have not been able communicate" (p. 6). This illustrates how there can be significant misunderstanding or gaps even in the same or similar cultures.

In every culture, linguistic metaphors are tools for understanding and can be meaningful and true. But the embodied gap exists somewhere between different cultures and sub-cultures (Lakoff and Johnson 1980). The gap between designer and user is, in most cases, essentially a cultural gap. For example, in designing interactive systems for healthcare, cultural (or sub-cultural) gaps can be found in several places, for example between patients and doctors, between elderly people and care givers, and between carers and health professionals.

We understand our physical experiences of the world, our spatial awareness, our bodily movement and the way we manipulate objects, through metaphors. In our everyday life, we spontaneously adopt a drooping posture when we come upon sadness in others or are ourselves living with depression. On the other hand, we adopt an erect posture when we feel positive emotional states. We sometime describe ourselves as '*feeling up*' or '*feeling down*' showing that we understand indefinite substance in terms of directionality relative to gravity (Lakoff and Johnson 1980). Lakoff and Johnson mention the fact that "we have bodies of the sort we have and they function as they do in our physical environment" (p. 14).

'Argument is war', spatialization and other metaphors take account of an embodied pre-linguistic structure of experience that motivates conceptual metaphor mapping, called an '*image schema*' (Johnson 1987). According to Lakoff (1987), image schemata are simple structures that constantly recur in our bodily experience, formed from our bodily interactions, from linguistic experience, and from historical context. Schemata have been applied in 'experiential' approaches to design. For example, Andreas Lund developed an information exploration environment called 'SchemaSpace' that sought to capture the human scale of people interacting with basic-level image schema categories, and through which interaction is experienced as natural both conceptually and perceptually (described in Lund 2003; Waterworth et al. 2003).

Image Schemata and Metaphorical Projection

We are animate beings who must interact with our environment. All such interaction requires the exertion of force either that is exerted on us passively or that we exert actively. Our experience is inseparable from forceful interaction. By focusing more on our experience of forceful interaction such as motion, directedness of action, degree of intensity, and structure of interaction and so on, human-primitives and their practical use in design process is disclosed.

Image Schemata

Johnson (1987) stressed that "forms of imaginative structuring of experience that grow out of bodily experience contribute to our understandings and guide our reasoning" (xiv). The human-experiential approach to design focuses on the structures of imaginative understanding that grow out of our embodied experience. Previously, human has been defined as: *People who share the same evolutionary history and hence, bodily structures and potential for experience and share the same primitives for understanding information.* The human primitives are a central concern to the human-experiential approach. Human primitives are imaginative structures, which consist of *image schemata* and *metaphorical projections*. According to Johnson (1987):

> A schema is a recurrent pattern, shape, and regularity in, or of, these ongoing ordering activities. These patterns emerge as meaningful structures for us chiefly at the level of our bodily movements through space, our manipulation of objects, and our perceptual interactions. (Johnson 1987, p. 29)

A number of image schemata of different types have been identified (e.g. Johnson 1987; Lakoff 1987; Hurtienne and Blessing 2007). Table 4.1 is a list of image schemata using the classification into seven types suggested by Hurtienne and Blessing (2007).

We, humans, develop image schemata, which are schematic structures of the patterns of embodied experience and perceptual structures of our sensibility through interacting with our environment such as our perception, bodily movement through

Table 4.1 Examples of image schemata

Image schema						
Basic	Space	Containment	Multiplicity	Process	Force	Attribute
Substance	Up-down	Container	Merging	Iteration	Diversion	Heavy-light
Object	Left-right	In-out	Collection	Cycle	Counterforce	Dark-bright
	Near-far	Content	Splitting		Restraint	Big-small
	Front-back	Full-empty	Part-whole		Removal	Warm-cold
	Centre-periphery	Surface	Count-mass		Resistance	Strong-weak
					Attraction	Straight
					Compulsion	Smooth-rough
	Contact		Link		Blockage	
	Path		Matching		Balance	
					Momentum	
	Scale				Enablement	

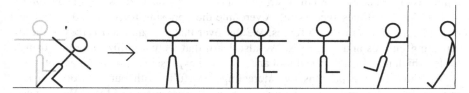

Fig. 4.1 Sensual experience of bodily balance

space, and physical manipulation of objects. Then grows the meaning of our specific notions of things. Sense is inseparably related to structuring meaning.

Let's look at the BALANCE schema that belongs to the Force group (Fig. 4.1) as an example, as elaborated by Johnson (1987). In the following we describe how our system of meaning is developed with patterns of typical experience of force, revealing the way in which image schemata work their way up into bodily expression, interaction and communication with our environment, which is the process that underlies human-experiential design.

Patterns Growing

Take an example of how a baby develops these patterns (Johnson 1987). When a baby is born, s/he begins to grasp the world around her/him through interacting with forces. Through the interactions with forces, patterned relations between her/his selves and the environment emerge repeatedly. The meaning of physical force is developed from such recurrent patterns. Owing to those recurrent patterns, a baby begins to grasp the world with a consistent order of relation.

Sensing can thus be viewed as an integral part of our understanding of the world around us from when we are born. We further experience a large number of perceptions and activities in everyday life, such as leaning with one's back against the wall or another person, perceiving stable structures in nature, perceiving slippery or non-skid textures, arranging books on a shelf and so on (Fig. 4.1). We then grasp this structure of BALANCE repeatedly through those experiences, images, and perception. Patterned recurring relations between ourselves and the environment develop into our meaning structures (Johnson 1987).

The BALANCE schema is embodied from activities in our perception, bodily experience through the environment, and physical manipulation of objects.

Patterns Expanding

Through various experiences of the world around us, we gradually gain and modify the meaning of and sense of *force* through bodily interactions. For example, we are often frustrated by "external and internal forces such as gravity, light, heat, wind, bodily processes, and the obtrusion of other physical objects" (Johnson 1987, p. 13). We sometimes successfully overcome the opposing force but often realize own impotence against such forces. We discover that we can exert forces in these repeating failures and successes. We also learn that we can utilize force by using tools, which may be a physical tool and even oral expressions that influence others.

We thus develop patterns by interacting forcefully with our environment by moving our bodies and manipulating objects as if we are centres of force. We are part of the environment and sources of force as well. Finally we learn skills from gross motor to fine motor control, such as using chopsticks, grabbing a cup or moving our bodies through space. In such fine and gross motor activities there are repeatable embodied patterns, which give coherent, intelligible, well-regulated and meaningful structure to our bodily experience at a pre-conceptual level.

Johnson (1987) suggests that:

> these embodied patterns do not remain private or peculiar to the person who experiences them. Our community helps interpret and codify many of our felt patterns. They become shared cultural modes of experience and help to determine the nature of our meaningful, coherent understanding of our world. (Johnson 1987, p. 14)

Emergence of the BALANCE Schema

Babies try to stand, to walk but unsteadily, and sometimes fall to the floor. They repeatedly try and fail until they open a new world of balanced standing posture. With our body, we sense when the balance is right, how to make adjustments and how the patterns of physical movement organize the proper patterns in constant activity. Through such sensual experiences of bodily balance, and of lack of balance, the meaning of balance is generated. We come to understand the notion of systemic balance in the pre-conceptual level through our bodily experience. According to Johnson (1987), an image schema such as BALANCE is not an image, not an object we can physically touch or see, and not a propositional structure or a conceptual rule. It is a way of giving order to structure particular experiences schematically so as to integrate our perceptions and conceptions.

So we learn the proper BALANCE of forces with our bodies through everyday activities. Learning BALANCE is something we do, not by grasping a set of abstract principles or conceptual thoughts. Any animate being must interact with the environment in order to survive. We interact with the environment, manipulate objects and we are affected by force. In all such interaction, we exert and experience forces. When we grasp the world around us, a central factor to comprehend our experience is the structure of force. Our experience and forceful activity cannot be separated.

We are rarely conscious of the presence of BALANCE, and almost never speculate on the nature and meaning of balance, because the experience of balance is pervasively infiltrated into everyday life and definitely fundamental to our coherent way of grasping our world. As Johnson (1987) expresses it: "the structure of balance is one of the key threads that holds our physical experience together as a relatively coherent and meaningful whole" (p. 74). The meaning of balance is interconnected to such experiences as our balancing in motion and systemic balance within our bodies, and to the image-schematic structures that make physical balancing coherent and meaningful for us. Because of the embodied image schemata, it is still recognizable through bodily experience, even if we have not yet learned concepts or externalized words for them.

Imagine that you lose your balance, as Fig. 4.1 shows. You slip and drop to the floor, then you try to get yourself back to an upright position. You recognize BALANCE in this activity. You attempt to distribute weight and forces appropriately around an imaginary vertical axis. The relevant physical forces have a significant role to establish BALANCE again. The 'imaginary' axis is an embodied recurrent pattern in the experience of balancing, not just a diagram illustrated on a paper (Fig. 4.2).

From the repeated experience of interacting forcefully with our environment, we generate the proper patterns of the 'imaginary' axis in constant activity to keep our bodies balanced in space (Fig. 4.2). The BALANCE schema can be expressed

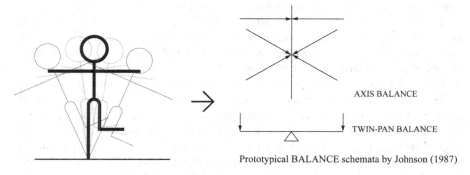

AXIS BALANCE

TWIN-PAN BALANCE

Prototypical BALANCE schemata by Johnson (1987)

Fig. 4.2 Imaginary axis and BALANCE schema

as force vectors and an upright axis or a point relative to which those forces are distributed. In any physical experience, balance organizes a symmetrical structure of forces around a point or axis. The prototypical schemata are modified so that the number of vectors is reduced to two symmetrical vectors and the number of points reduced to a simple point that forms a fulcrum (Fig. 4.2). The balanced and equal force vectors meet at this point.

The weave of our experience is interlaced with relations between various image-schematic structures. So image schemata are adaptable and flexibly modified to harmonize diverse situations. Image schemata are abstract representations and schematic gestalts in nature, not just symbols (Johnson 1987). The BALANCE schema, for example, is one of the recurrent dynamic patterns that emerge from bodily interactions that make up the way we grasp the world. They express the structural outlines of sensory-motor experience. They are embodied, and integrate information from various sensory systems and could be represented in a visual, haptic, kinaesthetic or acoustic manner through metaphorical projections.

Metaphorical Projections

Metaphorical projection is a cross-domain mapping of projecting patterns from one domain to another in order to support understanding of one concept in terms of another concept, where there is some similarity or correlation between them (Lakoff and Johnson 1980). Physical bodily experience works as a constraint to define the kinds of mappings that can emerge across domains.

Metaphor is not only a linguistic expression, but also, as Johnson (1987, v) stressed, "one of the chief cognitive structures by which we are able to have coherent, ordered experiences that we can reason about and make sense of". Patterns developed in our concrete bodily experience are employed in the form of metaphor to bring order to enable our more abstract understanding. Metaphorical projection from the concrete bodily experiences to the abstract domains helps understanding a world around us by making use of physical experience. Embodied schematic patterns are structured via various physical domains of bodily movements and interactions, and patterns can be projected by metaphor onto abstract domains.

The nature of metaphor reminds us the origin of the term 'design' in Latin, which is from de- 'out' + signare 'to mark,' from signum 'a mark, sign'. Design can be seen as bringing order to a chaotic state and to find a plan and conceive it in mind in 'order' to visualize or form something.

Figure 4.3 shows a stylistic interpretation of *"people who intuitively interpret what is of value for their purposes in their current environment and try to become harmonious with it in everyday life activities"* Goto et al. (2004). If there were no umbrella-stand available, people would stand the umbrella as Fig. 4.3 shows. The edge-point might be positioned in accordance with a feature of the environment, such as a slit between lines of floor tiles. The distance between the edge-point and the wall, the angle of the tilted umbrella and the force by which the umbrella stably stands-alone are perfectly meshed.

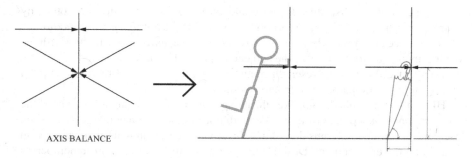

Fig. 4.3 Metaphorical projection as a trace of the natural flow of action

There exists a strong flow of action in this situation. This phenomenon can also be described as the behaviour drawn out by an *affordance* (Goto et al. 2004). Embodied realism also accounts for this phenomenon. To reveal the primitives during observation is to carefully see embodied and imaginative structures of understanding that emerge from our bodily experience at the present moment. Primitives appear in various forms of harmonious accord of physical environment and human body. There is a moment when the embodied meaning of physical forces emerges from our bodily experiences in everyday life.

In order to organize our more abstract understanding of the present moment in constant activity, we make use of embodied patterns that obtain through our physical experience. By metaphorical projection from the concrete to abstract, we are able to make the umbrella stand up with perfect distance from the wall, perfect height from the floor, and perfect angle of it (Fig. 4.3). This is an unconscious bodily experience that determines the kind of mapping that transfers across domains. Metaphorical projection moves from the bodily sense (with its emergent schema) to grasping the world around us at the present moment. On this base, we should be able to see how it is that our experience of bodily balance, and of the perception of balance, is connected to our understanding of a balanced current state of being in the world.

Implications for Human-Experiential Design

It is not easy to reveal such primitives by ordinary user research using techniques such as video taping, interviewing or shadowing. The human-experiential approach puts design back into embodied everyday experience. User observation in human-experiential design should be conducted to lead us back from conceptual methods, preconceived ideas and abstract forms, to the situation of experience itself. It helps design to be embedded into experience and to disappear from perception, and this supports the natural flow of action with no conscious effort. Ironically, we don't remember when we are present in the natural flow of action and how we behave in the flow. Prejudice and preoccupation with self-identity become a hindrance for designers and researchers to see reality. It is important to divest the self and release the tenacious attitude of being oneself.

The key is to realise that designer and user are connected to each other by sharing primitives arising from embodiment and the experience of embodiment. Designers need to observe human primitives that are revealed in interacting with the environment, but not to observe the subject as a user. This is somewhat distant from a variety of ordinary user research methods such as contextual research, applied ethnography, participatory design and so on.

Human-experiential design takes the perspective of user as human and part of the environment, not separate from it. The mediator in this approach integrates design, user and environment. It thus denies the objectivist view of humans as separate from others and the environment. Design as mediator should help to us in remembering the wholeness we have forgotten. The mediator is not merely a middleman or a facilitator, but has a major role in which we can answer the question of what it means to be human from the design point of view.

Blends and What They Add to Metaphors

As Lakoff and Johnson (1980) describe it a *conceptual metaphor* refers to the understanding of one idea or conceptual domain, in terms of another. It is a cross-domain mapping, taking elements from one domain and applying them to another. The conceptual domains hypothesized in conceptual metaphors have two main roles: source and target. For example, English expressions like "*My computer is a desktop*", which could be taken as a desktop metaphor of a PC.

- '*Desktop*' is the source domain from which we bring metaphorical expressions (My computer is *a desktop*).
- '*My computer*' is the target domain that we try to understand and experience (*My computer* is a desktop).

"*My computer is a desktop*" offers the primitive material for understanding new concepts. However, it does not directly indicate "a desktop interface of a PC." The desktop metaphor of a PC is actually a newly emergent space – a *blend*. According to Imaz and Benyon (2006), "if the metaphor is a cross-domain mapping, taking elements from one domain and applying them to another, then blending is an operation that is applied to two input spaces, and which results in a new, blended space" (p. 43). Blending is the ability to take two mental spaces, and connect them in certain ways such that a blended mental space emerges, and this is the ability that gives rise to the possibility of art, science, and language (Fauconnier and Turner 2002).

In the terminology of blending theory, the concept of mental space refers to partial cognitive structures that emerge when we think and talk (Fauconnier 1997). According to Fauconnier (1997), there is a process of mental synthesis where previous experiences, cultural contexts and historical events are brought together to act in the form of frames or schemata, in between language and the real world. Mental spaces are set up and built on from many sources. 'Connectors' link mental

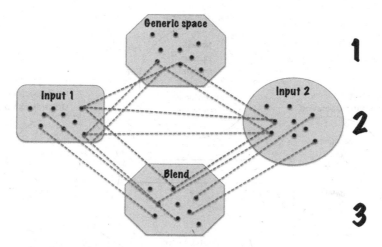

Fig. 4.4 Generic space and blended space

spaces to one another (Fig. 4.4). A mapping between an element of one space and one or more elements of another is established by means of a connector.

As shown in Fig. 4.4, using standard figurative representations originally used by Fauconnier and Turner (2002), connectors link elements of two spaces, a source mental space and a target mental space. Mental spaces are established, structured, and linked to other spaces. Blending works as follows:

1. Generic space: reflects abstract structure and organization shared by the inputs, and defines the core cross-space mapping between them.
2. Cross-space mapping: elements and relations between two input spaces are connected.
3. Blend: a new emergent structure not provided directly by the inputs.

Conceptual metaphor and conceptual blending are both about the idea of projection of structure between domains, but since conceptual blending is focused on new conceptualizations, the newly emergent space is often different from the real world we normally experience. The gap between a user and an interactive system, because of which users still struggle to use or understand newly released systems even though technologies have been evolving steadily, can be seen as caused by this issue.

Desktop Interface as Blend

The WIMP-based graphical user interfaces have become a blend rather than a metaphor for something else, since the notion now represents a new emergent space (Imaz and Benyon 2006) – a thing in itself as far as cognition is concerned. The

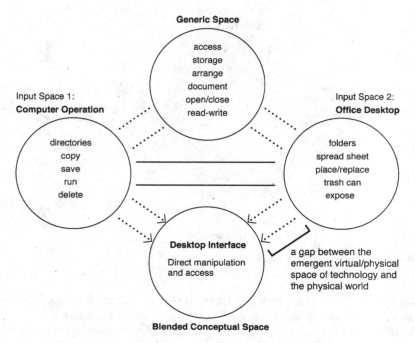

Fig. 4.5 PC "desktop" as blend

WIMP-based GUI with a desktop metaphor has been through a long process of evolution. We no longer see computer windows in the blended conceptual space as similar to real windows or interface menus as similar to menus in a restaurant (Imaz and Benyon 2006).

Figure 4.5 shows how blending works with the PC desktop. Two input spaces, input space-1 and input space-2 exist and the solid lines indicate a cross-space mapping that connects elements and relations between these inputs. The two principal inputs have different organizing frames. Input space-1 refers to the frame of traditional computer operations, and input space-2 refers to the frame of office work. The dotted lines refer to connections between inputs and either generic or blended space. A generic space maps on to each of the inputs and contains what the inputs have in common, which reflects some more abstract structure and organization they share.

The blended conceptual space is one possible emergent conceptual structure containing new ideas and insights. The emergent property of the blend provides direct manipulation and access. In the interfaces using the 'desktop metaphor' with direct manipulation and access, the grasping, releasing, and opening of an object are imitated by dragging, dropping, and double clicking on perceivable icons, objects and folders on the virtual surface. These are new emergent functions that exist neither in the real world nor the domain of computer operations. They appear in the blended conceptual space. Because of this newly emergent space, the experience is very distinctive from physical experience in everyday life.

This blend is powerful and as been successful in opening up the use of computers to a mass market. But it is also limiting and is not understandable for many of the new situations and possibilities opened up by new technologies, especially as they permeate the physical world in the form of mixed realities, and are used by an ever wider variety of people, in different cultures and subcultures. In these new situations, there emerges a clear gap between the new blended space and the physical world of action in which we naturally function. At the least, users encounter a physical-virtual gap that disrupts the flow of action during activities that require a changeover between the physical and the virtual. They are forced into conscious efforts to access information and carry out intentions.

In the next chapter (Chap. 5), we present out solution for bridging these contextual reality gaps by applying human-experiential design in the creation of blended reality spaces.

References

Chalmers M, MacColl I (2003) Seamful and seamless design in Ubiquitous computing. Workshop at the crossroads: the interaction of HCI and systems issues in Ubicomp. Ubicomp 2003 Seattle

Fauconnier G (1997) Mappings in thought and language. Cambridge University Press, Cambridge

Fauconnier G, Turner M (2002) The way we think: conceptual blending and the mind's hidden complexities. Basic Books, New York

Goto T, Sasaki M, Fukasawa N (2004) The ecological approach to design. Tokyo shoseki, Tokyo

Hurtienne J, Blessing L (2007) Design for intuitive use – testing image schema theory for user interface design. Paper presented at the international conference on engineering design, ICED'07

Imaz M, Benyon D (2006) Designing with blends: conceptual foundations of human-computer interaction and software engineering. The MIT Press, Cambridge, MA

Ishii H (2008) Tangible Bits: beyond pixels. Paper presented at the 2nd international conference on tangible and embedded interaction, Kingston

Jacob RJK, Girouard A, Hirshfield LM, Horn MS, Shaer O, Solovey ET, et al (2007) Reality-Based interaction: unifying the new generation of interaction styles. Paper presented at the CHI'07 extended abstracts on Human factors in computing systems. ACM Press

Johnson M (1987) The body in the mind: the bodily basis of meaning, imagination and reason. University of Chicago Press, Chicago

Lakoff G (1987) Woman, fire and dangerous things: what categories reveal about the mind. The University of Chicago Press, Chicago

Lakoff G, Johnson M (1980) Metaphors we live by. The University of Chicago Press, Chicago

Lund A (2003) Massification of the intangible: a investigation into embodied meaning and information visualization. PhD thesis, Umeå University, Sweden

Nelson T (1999) The folly of "Metaphors". http://xanadu.com.au/ted/TN/WRITINGS/TCOMPARADIGM/tedCompOneLiners.html. Accessed 12 Dec 2015

Polanyi M (1966) The tacit dimension. The University of Chicago Press, Chicago

Rogers Y, Scaife M, Gabrielli S, Smith H, Harris E (2002) A conceptual framework for mixed reality environments: designing novel learning activities for young children. Presence 11(6):677–686

Waterworth JA, Lund A, Modjeska D (2003) Experiential design of shared information spaces. In: Höök K, Benyon D, Munro AJ (eds) Designing information spaces: the social navigation approach. Springer, Great Britain, pp 125–149

Chapter 5
Bridging Contextual Gaps with Blended Reality Spaces

Abstract The major barrier to easily used and understood interactive technology is often a contextual reality gap between users and designers, and between different classes of user. In this chapter we discuss the importance of context in understanding communications and provide examples of problems arising from a lack of shared context. We then outline the potential of blended reality spaces to bridge contextual reality gaps between the physical world and the virtual and so provide a shared space for presence, communication and action. As long as we can act in the physical world, we can enact intentions related to the virtual – if the blended space is successfully designed. We go on to suggest that, through human-experiential design, the blended reality approach can be extended to a range of application areas, including health care and rehabilitation.

Introduction

Making sense of any communication and of many interactive situations depends on sharing a context, except in those rare situations when only context-free explicit statements are exchanged – as at times in a court of law. In all other situations, and throughout our lives, we use context unconsciously to make sense of what is happening and what others are saying. The major barrier to easily used and understood interactive technology is often a contextual reality gap between users and designers, and between different classes of user. Increasingly often, the introduction of embedded and worn technology into the physical environment opens up contextual reality gaps when users try to function in both. Blended reality spaces are designed to bridge this gap and provide a shared space for presence, communication and action.

As in all blend-based design (see Chap. 4), in designing blended reality spaces we combine aspects of one input space with those of another – to arrive at a new integrated reality that has the potential to eventually stand as a thing-in-itself in our understanding. When designing blended reality spaces, one of the input spaces is the physical world, and the product of our design process is a reality that blends aspects

© Springer International Publishing Switzerland 2016
J. Waterworth, K. Hoshi, *Human-Experiential Design of Presence in Everyday Blended Reality*, Human–Computer Interaction Series,
DOI 10.1007/978-3-319-30334-5_5

of the physical with selected possibilities from the digital. The challenge is to arrive at something coherent and that makes sense in the situations in which people wish to function.

A unitary sense of presence, mediated by both technology and the physical world, is a defining feature of blended reality spaces and affords an intimate linking of intentions with actions (Riva et al. 2011). As long as we can act in the physical world, we can enact intentions related to the virtual – if the blended space is successfully designed. In most current mixed realities our sense of presence, of being somewhere, is split between the physical world and the virtual environments created by technology, as we discussed in Chap. 1. But when tangibility is incorporated in the right way as an element of interaction, a more integrated sense of mediated presence – *tangible presence* – in what is effectively a blended reality space becomes possible. Such a space supports shareable presence in a physical-digital reality.

In the remainder of this chapter we discuss the importance of context in understanding communications and outline the potential of blended reality spaces to bridge contextual reality gaps. From this we go on to suggest that the blended reality approach can be extended to a range of application areas, including health care and rehabilitation. In the next chapter (Chap. 6), we present examples of the approach applied to the design of a variety of illustrative everyday life contexts.

The Importance of Context

Contemporary information and communication technology has broken through many boundaries between cultures, societies and even political systems, but has not yet overcome the communicational boundaries that arise from a lack of shared understanding, a contextual reality gap. Understanding how people really are is difficult in cross-cultural communication. We unfortunately tend to blame 'people of different cultures', for their apparent "stupidity, deceit, or craziness" (Hall 1969, ix), when it is actually obvious that we often just don't understand people from different contexts than our own.

How can interactive systems effectively help with bridging the reality gap generated between different users' perceptions in different contexts? In order to explore where the sharing of reality is restricted or concealed, we need to investigate more closely everyday life communication that creatively and effectively enables mutual understandings between people. Everyday communication contains hidden resources for creating harmonious accord of people and things that can be applied in interaction design.

Communication is commonly assumed to involve a meaningful linguistic exchange. However, when we look carefully at everyday communication between families, close friends and loved ones, they communicate rather like a synchronized instrument, each anticipating the wishes of the other, making communication without or with little explicit information. Imagine, for example, when a child comes home from her/his school, sits on a sofa, has a soft drink with gulping, summarizes her/his feelings about the way things went at the classroom. If her/his mother wants the details, s/he may have to listen for a while, yet she perceives in an instant a significant message about her child, with implications for what kind of evening they are going to spend.

Polanyi (1966) in his book 'The Tacit Dimension', brought out the importance of what people know but cannot externalize, what he called tacit knowledge. The hidden meanings contained in silence and blank intervals are manifest to our sensory perception. Communication relies on how well people provide and utilize the 'empty space' flexibly to form their own images to fill the spaces in sensory perception, and how well we accept the images of each other.

Empty space is an important component of communication. It has a multiplicity of meanings and signifies both temporal and spatial principles, an interval of space and time. It can be the specific time that characterizes an interval of music or dance (Hosoe et al. 1991). It exists in the visual arts, architecture and the urban environment as well. For example, space itself is perceived entirely differently between cultures. In some cultures, especially Japanese culture, spaces are perceived, named, and even revered as the 'MA', or intervening interval. In Western culture, people more often perceive the objects but not the spaces between them (Hall 1959). They pay attention to the object arrangement. In contrast, in Japan, it is the arrangement of the spaces that is most salient (Hosoe et al. 1991). Many scientists, architects, space designers, communication designers and artists have paid attention to this phenomenon (Hosoe et al. 1991; Hall 1969; Hara 2009). The empty time and space opens and closes, swells and contracts. It gives us new ways of solution, creation and communication through constant attention to the use of space as though it gave abilities with no constraints on functional flexibility (Hosoe et al. 1991).

Recently interaction designers have paid greater attention to ambient information in everyday life. For example, people also communicate with the natural sources of ambient information to interpret how things are around them in everyday life. This communication is not linguistic conceptual exchange, but rather people intuitively interpreting what is of value for their purposes in their current environment and trying to become harmonious with it in everyday life activities. But, "this ability to convey ideas does not transfer well to humans interacting via computer" (Dey 2001). Communication and collaboration through conventional computer and telecommunication systems diminishes the qualities of interaction that produce a sense of directness and richness, because of their limited capacity to convey a reality with contexts shared between users (Hoshi and Waterworth 2008). Context is an important source of information in designing interactive systems, however not yet effectively utilized (Dey 2001; Salber et al. 1999).

The Contextual Reality Framework

Hall (1969) has described the phenomenon of "empty space" in communication using a different term. What he terms *high-context communication* is where "the communication or messages is one in which most of the information is either in

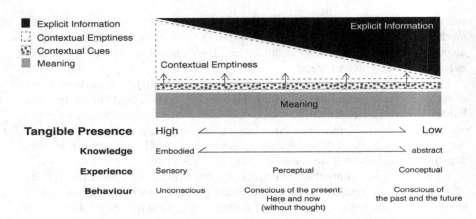

Fig. 5.1 The contextual reality framework

the physical context or internalized in the person" (p. 91), whereas low-context communication is where the information is vested in explicit code through words and verbalization, just as two lawyers in a courtroom during a trial. The closer the relationship the more high-context communication arises, drawing on shared meaning. But how do we derive 'meaning' from the empty space internalized in the person, while the coded, explicit, transmitted part of the message conveys very little?

Figure 5.1, building on the hi-low context continuum originally proposed by Hall (1976), represents our concept of *the Contextual Reality Framework* and shows how emptiness and meaning have a strong relation established through this communicative process.

Context refers to the conditions in which a communication exists that make its meaning understandable. Meaning, hence, can be clarified by such *contextual cues* as the surroundings, circumstances, environment, background, or setting. More specifically, subtle cues such as weight, texture, smell, airflow, sound, light and so on contribute to context. A *contextual cue* is a catalyst that facilitates creativity through *sensory experience*. According to Krippendorff (2005), "Sense is the feeling of being in contact with the world without reflection, interpretation, or explanation" (p. 50). Naturally synchronized communication in everyday life largely relies on the unconscious affirmation of the sense of being filled up and/or filling up emptiness with contextual cues.

Perceptual experience is a group of sensations automatically retained and integrated by percepts, which gives it the ability to capture the current state of being in a world. It takes place externally, in the present, the here and now, neither in the past nor in the future (Riva et al. 2004). Our bodily involvement with perceived objects and our perception of objects are inseparable. We become harmonized to things that all of us end up doing without really thinking. It is meaningless to think of mind, body, and context separately.

Conceptual experience is based on information processing such as problem-solving, analysing, thinking what happened in the past and what can be expected to happen in the future (Riva et al. 2004). It invokes conscious mental behaviour expressed with verbal communication and an imagined body. It is the process of mental realization including sense, perception, memory and even judgment. Hence, it is not easy to make a clear distinction between *sensory, perceptual and conceptual experience*. They should be integrated appropriately in a particular situation. As Lakoff and Johnson (1980) pointed out, "It is as though the ability to comprehend experience through metaphors were sense, like seeing or touching or hearing, with metaphors providing the only ways to perceive and experience much of the world" (p. 239).

Contextual Reality Gaps

Many professional domains, for example in healthcare or the law, require abstract and objective data, with explicit expression. In contrast, their patients or clients have different needs and characteristics and form their understandings within a completely different operating context. As an example, the contextual reality gap between elderly people at home and professional people in the healthcare domain is illustrated in Fig. 5.2.

More and more patients are treated and taken care of in their own homes instead of in hospitals or specialist care centres (Winge et al. 2005). This fact suggests new types of requirement on the staff and increases the importance of well functioning communication and collaboration between the different caregivers, and between them and the care receivers, in order to create appropriate care services (Winge and Waterworth 2014). The standard interface of the 'desktop metaphor', using a keyboard, a mouse, and a small computer screen is so familiar that it is sometimes

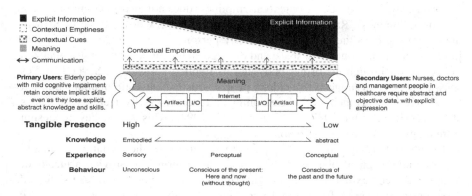

Fig. 5.2 The contextual reality gap between people at home and professional people in the healthcare domain

hard to imagine other approaches. But even though it works well in some situations – such as typical office work – it is not at all suitable in many other situations, and especially not for people with special needs, such as those with mental/physical disabilities and elderly people with dementia who lose explicit skills and the ability to understand abstract knowledge.

How can interactive systems effectively help with bridging the contextual reality gap generated between different users' perceptions in different contexts? These needs could potentially be addressed in several ways, in particular using the right information 'context' and creating the sense of being together with other people in a shared mediated environment. By effectively bridging the contextual reality gap, interactive systems could provide the richest communication, thus making it possible to create more effective collaborative environments that enrich the sense of being together with other participants for healthcare in remote locations. For this to be successful, it is vitally important to pursue a design approach that originates in the pursuit of the senses for specific users and situations, particularly in the case of those who have difficulties dealing with abstract information.

Modern societies are quite safely equipped with numerous implementations for people's health, both at health services and in homes. But in practice, these carefully designed medical information systems and products often hardly work at all. This is not due to the technology itself, but rather because of design and implementation processes without an appropriate human-centred point of view. For decades, most healthcare system failures have been due to the lack of true human-centredness, even though e-health technologies have been evolving steadily (Zhang 2008). Substantial information is not only to be found in such explicit information as words or charts. People feel it with their bodies, as sensory perceptions. Krippendorff refers to Gibson's ecological approach to perception that "The process of constructing the meaning relies on the human ability to act so as to change an existing sense to a preferred one" (p. 53).

An elderly person living at home intuitively interprets what is of value for their purposes in their current environment and tries to become harmonious with it in everyday life activities. Contextual-emptiness does not mean a communication lack or nothingness. Rather, it indicates a condition that will likely be filled with the contextual cues they prefer. The elderly person comes to understand implicit information in this contextual space and distinguish the hidden meanings contained in it directly, through his or her body and its implicit knowledge. Several studies show evidence that suggests that elderly people with dementia still maintain implicit knowledge, even as their explicit reasoning and memory skills decline (e.g. Zacks et al. 2007; Schacter 1987; Benjamin et al. 1994). This is the key to design technology that is accessible to all.

By understanding what makes sense to the users in their context of being, experiential design of blended reality space can in principle provide a means of bridging the contextual reality gap. This approach does not require users' forced reasoning to interpret information. By looking at an empty vessel, not as a negative state, but in terms of its capacity to be filled with contextual cues, the risk of a reality gap will be reduced. The sharing of meaning, usually restricted or concealed because of limited capacity of conveying explicit information, will be released.

Bridging Contextual Gaps Through Blended Reality Spaces

In most current mixed realities our sense of presence, of being somewhere, is split between the physical world and the virtual environments created by technology. Tangibility has been suggested as an approach to this problem (e.g. Ishii 2008) and in the HCI literature it is described as being built upon sophisticated skills situating digital information, to varying extents, in physical space. But the approach is subject to our current limited abilities to represent changes in material or physical properties of objects and spaces (Hoshi et al. 2009). We often find a lack of tangibility in our everyday lives with digital artefacts. At the same time, our everyday lives are increasingly pervaded with digital information from environmentally built-in media devices such as high definition displays, automated systems and sensor-based environments. Further, information surrounding us is often displayed in the periphery as well as to the focus of our attention.

It is vitally important that the emerging trend towards tangibility is provided using the most appropriate combinations of the physical and virtual. This is especially true for people with special needs in their everyday lives, which is the main motivation for our work in this area. Blended reality spaces, evoking optimal tangible presence, carry the potential to make full use of, while not overburdening, the flexible but limited capacities of selective attention.

In the terminology of blend theory, blended reality spaces can be described as new emergent spaces that are immersive, interactive and body-movement oriented, and where there will be little or no conscious effort of action or access to information. The user perceives and acts directly, as in everyday life unmediated activities (Fig. 5.3). We see the first examples of this in some commercial games that have been successfully applied to training people with sensorimotor disorder or with cognitive dementia.

In typical examples of both Nintendo's Wii™(Nintendo Inc., Kyoto, Japan) and some video-capture games, the players have no direct physical connection with the game environment. Their physical movements are detected by either the 'Wiimote' (the Wii remote control) or by a camera. Body movements carried out by players are done in response to game-initiated events. When their free body movements in physical space are tracked and used as inputs to the game, a truly merged physical/media space is created during play, and this is a blended reality space. This interaction style is formed in the harmony between the physical and the virtual, utilizing tangible interaction. In a true blending of the physical and the virtual there will be little or no gap between the emergent virtual/physical space of technology and the physical world (Fig. 5.1).

Adopting the PACT (people, activities, contexts, and technologies) framework for HCI introduced by Benyon et al. (2004), blended reality space can be described as in Fig. 5.4. It is about harmonizing these four elements within various domains. We believe that true blended reality space will release human actions from physical constraints and the physical-virtual disruption, and provide natural a flow of actions, equivalent to those in the physical world.

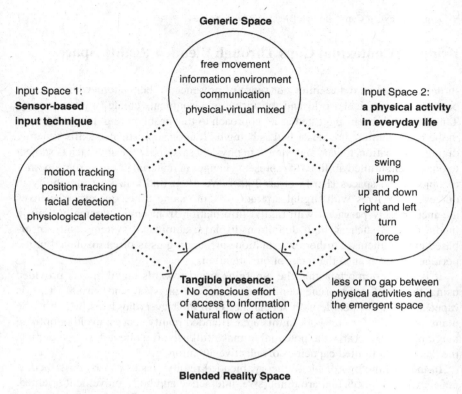

Fig. 5.3 Tangible presence in blended reality space

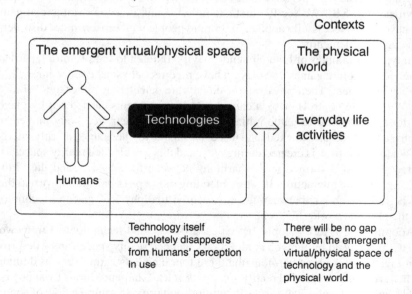

Fig. 5.4 Blended reality space expressed in the terms of the people, activities, contexts, and technologies (PACT) framework

Achieving true blended reality is not easy, for many reasons – not least the singularity of physical space and the multiplicities of the virtual. In current, partially blended gaming spaces, there exists the potential to give players a more immersive and physically challenging gaming situation, which can be expected to also produce a strong psychological feeling of presence (as the perceptual illusion of non-mediation; Lombard and Ditton 1997) within the merged space, since the technology effectively disappears from attention. This in turn may facilitate players' performance and maintain motivation and interest in the game.

Tangibility and Co-presence in Blended Reality Space

The strength of the sense of integrated presence in a blended reality is indicative of the degree of success in blending the physical and the digital successfully, to bridge the contextual reality gap. The inclusion of tangible objects and of other persons in a reality increases the changes of evoking a high level integrated presence.

Conceptualizations of presence can roughly be divided into two broad categories, physical and social (Lombard and Ditton 1997). Physical presence refers to the sense of being physically located in mediated space, whereas social presence refers to the feeling of being together with another person, of social interaction with a virtual or remotely located communication partner. IN the common ground of these two categories, there is a shared space uniting rich characteristics of both physical and social presence. That is defined as a sense of being together, co-presence (Ijsselsteijn and Riva 2003; see Fig. 5.5).

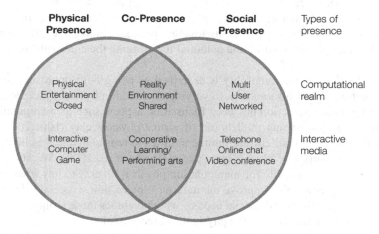

Fig. 5.5 Different types of presence

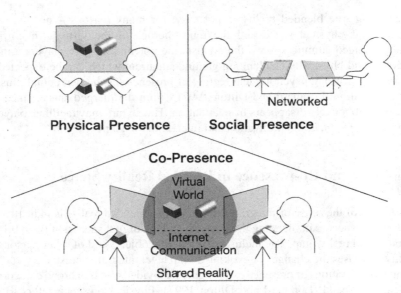

Fig. 5.6 Physical and virtual worlds correspond with each other to create the sense of being together between remote sites

Figure 5.5 graphically illustrates the different types of presence, including physical presence, social presence and co-presence, particularly in relation to the current computational realm, with interactive media examples.

Social presence in Fig. 5.6 is the case where traditional networked communication disconnects between the physical and the computational realm. Co-presence in Fig. 5.6 illustrates where the physical world and the virtual world correspond to each other to create the sense of being together between remote sites. By sharing a blended virtual-physical world, the potential for bridging the contextual reality gap is created.

In the HCI literature, tangibility is described as being built upon sophisticated skills situating digital information, to varying extents, in physical space. Research work on tangible interaction has been focused on aspects such as manipulation of building blocks or shaping models out of virtual/physical clay (Ishii 2008). The approach is subject to our current limited abilities to represent changes in material or physical properties of objects and spaces (Hoshi et al. 2009). We still cannot effectively utilize our skills for manipulating physical objects to any great extent, skills that are predicted to improve the nature of interaction, especially for people with mental and/or physical special needs – which includes those struggling to cope with competing demands from the physical and the virtual.

The quality of interaction that produces the sense of presence depends on how effectively a reality with its own contexts, *contextual reality*, is conveyed in the blended reality space, and shared between users in communication and collaboration. The more appropriate sensual perception is created during interaction in blended reality space, the more tangible co-presence users feel.

Effective blended reality systems must work by creating harmony through using appropriate contexts and thus creating optimal presence states. Contextual cues about colour, material, shape, size, texture, and weight configuration of the physical object provide possible improvement in a blended reality environment. Haptic feedback helps users feel a degree of tangibility, a convergence between the physical and virtual. But while haptic feedback can contribute, tangibility is not the same as haptics, in the same way that experienced presence is not the same as technologically-induced immersion (Waterworth et al. 2015).

Tangible presence and co-presence are about supporting a natural flow of action and almost unconscious sense of the here and now, within shareable contexts. This is the potential experience of those interacting within blended reality spaces. The next chapter (Chap. 6) provides several illustrative examples of the human-experiential design of such blended reality spaces.

References

Benjamin LT, Hopkins JR, Nation JR (1994) Psychology, 3rd edn. Macmillan College Publishing Company, New York

Benyon D, Turner P, Turner S (2004) Designing interactive systems: people, activities, context, technologies. Pearson Education, Maidenhead

Dey AK (2001) Understanding and using context. Personal Ubiquit Comput 5(1):4–7

Hall ET (1959) The silent language. Bantam Doubleday Dell Publishing Group, Garden City

Hall ET (1969) The hidden dimension. Anchor, Doubleday, Garden City

Hall ET (1976) Beyond culture. Anchor, Doubleday, Garden City

Hara K (2009) White. Lars Muller Publishers, Baden

Hoshi K, Waterworth JA (2008) Effective collaboration for healthcare by bridging the reality gap across media-physical spaces. Paper presented at the proceedings of the 1st international conference on PErvasive technologies related to assistive environments

Hoshi K, Pesola U-M, Waterworth EL, Waterworth J (2009) Tools, perspectives and avatars in blended reality space. In Weiderhold BK, Riva G (eds) Annual international CyberTherapy and CyberPsychology 2009. Italy, June 2009. IOS Press, Amsterdam

Hosoe I, Marinelli A, Sias R (1991) Play office: toward a new culture in the workplace. GC inc, Tokyo

Ijsselsteijn WA, Riva G (2003) Being there: the experience of presence in mediated environments. In: Riva G, Davide F, IJsselsteijn WA (eds) Being there: concepts, effects and measurement of user present in synthetic environments. Ios Press, Amsterdam, pp 3–16, 344

Ishii H (2008) Tangible bits: beyond pixels. Paper presented at the The 2nd international conference on tangible and embedded interaction, Kingston, ON, Canada

Krippendorff K (2005) The semantic turn: a new foundation for design. CRC press, Taylor & Francis Group, Boca Raton

Lakoff G, Johnson M (1980) Metaphors we live by. The University of Chicago Press, Chicago

Lombard M, Ditton T (1997) At the heart of it all: the concept of presence. J Comput Mediated-Commun. http://onlinelibrary.wiley.com/doi/10.1111/j.1083-6101.1997.tb00072.x/abstract

Polanyi M (1966) The tacit dimension. The University of Chicago Press, Chicago

Riva G, Waterworth JA, Waterworth EL (2004) The layers of presence: a bio-cultural approach to understanding presence in natural and mediated environments. Cyberpsychol Behav 7(4): 402–416

Riva G, Waterworth JA, Waterworth EL, Mantovani F (2011) From intention to action: the role of presence. New Ideas Psychol 29(1):24–37

Salber D, Dey AK, Abowd GD (1999) The context toolkit: aiding the development of context-enabled applications. Paper presented at the proceedings of the SIGCHI conference on Human factors in computing systems: the CHI is the limit

Schacter DL (1987) Implicit memory: history and current status. J Exp Psychol Learn Mem Cogn 13:501–518

Waterworth JA, Waterworth EL, Riva G, Mantovani F (2015) Presence: form, content and consciousness. In Lombard M, Biocca F, Freeman J, IJsselsteijn W, Schaevitz RJ (eds) Immersed in media: telepresence theory, measurement & technology. Springer, Switzerland. ISBN: 978-3-319-10189-7

Winge M, Waterworth EL (2014) Scenario for a patient at home in health and social care. Healthc Leadersh, ISSN 1179-3201, 6:51–66

Winge M, Waterworth EL, Augustsson N-P, Fors U, Wangler B (2005) Exploring the concept of patient-centred collaboration in health care – a study of home care in two Swedish cities. Paper presented at the The 10th international symposium on health information management research

Zacks RT, Hasher L, Li KZH (2007) Human memory. In: Craik FIM, Salthouse TA (eds) The handbook of aging and cognition. LEA, Hillsdale, pp 293–358

Zhang J (2008) Human-centred computing in health information systems, Part 1: analysis and design. J Biomed Inform 38(1):1–3

Part III
Blending Reality

This Part of the book provides several case histories of real life situations that can be seen as early examples of physical/digital blending, bringing out in a practical way the value of human-experiential design. Finally, we speculate about further developments and provide a vision of a future where we all live and function in a blended reality that is both physical and digital.

Chapter 6
Designing Blended Reality Spaces

Abstract This chapter explores how the human-experiential design approach can make it possible to smoothly blend perception and action, and apply it to the nature of designing embodied interaction. The approach attempts to make progress towards an ideal in which our activities are characterized by a natural flow of action, without significant intrusion from technology, across the physical-virtual divide. The resulting tangible sense of presence in blended reality spaces can be applied in a variety of everyday settings. Here we explore some of them, including a home-based system for the physical and psychosocial wellbeing of elderly people. In essence, human-experiential design combines practical aspects, related to human-computer interaction (HCI), with more experiential aspects relating to factors affecting the sense of presence in a location, to capitalize on implicit skills by utilizing real world objects that people are familiar with.

Introduction

Human-experiential design of physical-digital blends has the potential to impact on our everyday lives in several different but interrelated ways. In this chapter we present three examples to bring out different aspects of this impact (while also stressing their essential interrelatedness) in terms of our minds, our bodies, our social life and the world in which we live.

The way in which we perceive and function with our bodies – our sense of our own embodiment in relation to the world around us (including physical and digital aspects) – is changed when we perceive ourselves acting from the altered perspectives provided by technology. Depending on how *altered embodiment* (Waterworth and Waterworth 2014) is designed, this can impede or assist us in dealing with mixed reality. We start with the simplest case of a blended reality space, a sensor-based physical-virtual game. An experiment involving altered embodiment as an avatar in games is presented, focusing on how design aspects (viewpoint, avatar characteristics) affect user self-perceptions and behavioural reactions. A further example related to child physiotherapy illustrates the value of the approach for specific applications.

© Springer International Publishing Switzerland 2016
J. Waterworth, K. Hoshi, *Human-Experiential Design of Presence in Everyday Blended Reality*, Human–Computer Interaction Series, DOI 10.1007/978-3-319-30334-5_6

Our mental activities are also changed through physical-digital blending, along with some of the ways in which we carry out our intentions. An integrated sense of mediated presence can potentially provide a smoother link between our intentions and actions in any combined physical/virtual situation, including those for users who are not familiar with current technology. The example of a designed system for tangible social networking for the elderly is presented, as a case of satisfying special needs via what we see as an almost universal approach to design.

A Blended Reality Game

Blended reality space is essentially an interactive environment where the physical and the virtual are intimately combined. A number of researchers have experimented with sensor-based techniques for interacting with virtual entities via the manipulation of physical objects in space. The main idea of such a tangible interface, built on movement and position sensing techniques, is to provide physical forms which serve as both representations of and controls to digital information. The applications make it possible to directly manipulate the digital information with our hands, and perceptible through our peripheral senses through physical embodiment (Ishii 2008; Ishii and Ullmer 1997; Ullmer and Ishii 2000). Through this physical-virtual combination, physical objects provide users with clues about the virtual environment and help them develop skills in that environment, such as picking up, positioning, altering, and arranging objects (Ishii 2008). This definition provides a common understanding of the concept, but it does not identify the factors influencing the sense of presence in such spaces, nor does it describe the exact nature of the experience.

What aspects does blended reality space contribute to the experience of presence? Motivated by this question, we carried out an experimental study that examined three key factors in the way blended realities may be implemented (reported in more detail in Hoshi and Waterworth 2009):

- The extent to which tangible tools play a role in interaction
- Whether a first person or a third person perspective is provided from the user's point of view; and
- If a third person perspective (of a self-representing avatar) is used, how closely the representation matches the appearance of the user.

We used the Nintendo Wii video game and console, commonly available and widely used technology that can provide a satisfying and involving gaming experience even with relatively inexpensive technology, including computer graphics with quite low resolution.

The experiment looked at the effect of these variables on rated presence (Lombard and Ditton 1997) and also *self-presence* (Ratan et al. 2007), which is the defined as the extent to which a person experiences a sense of identity with a virtual characterisation of themselves – an avatar. Our expectation was that a physical tool would enhance the sense of presence. Avatars provide a concrete representation of the player's actions and identity (Borberg et al. 2008; Castranova 2003; Becker and Mark 2001) and so we expected that there would be both higher presence and self-presence when the avatar resembled the player more accurately. We also expected that using a tool would produce higher presence than not using a tool.

A first person perspective duplicates the natural view of ones own actions by providing interaction with the blended reality space as if from the players' own physical viewpoint (Waterworth and Waterworth 2008). With a third person perspective, in contrast, they see their own representation as a representation of themselves – an avatar – whose bodily movements reflect their physical movements in real time (Waterworth and Waterworth 2008). Because of this difference, we expected a stronger feeling of presence to be elicited with a first person perspective than with a third person perspective.

To test these expectations, we created several different versions of blended reality space, based on the Nintendo Wii gaming environment, its wireless movement-sensing Wiimote interaction device, and a 60" plasma display (as shown in Fig. 6.1). For the present study, a simple avatar-oriented game was chosen that provides a third person view (Wii tennis) and another simple game that provides a first person view (Kororinpa).

Wii tennis requires a swinging motion of the handheld Wiimote to hit the virtual ball, while Kororinpa requires more delicate hand movements of the device to guide a marble through virtual mazes.

As can be seen in Figs. 6.1 and 6.2, we embedded the Wiimote in a physical tennis racquet or maze board. For the no tool conditions the Wiimote was worn in a glove on the back of the participant's dominant hand. In the third person view conditions, the avatar used was either the pre-supplied one (identical for all participants) or was one designed by each participant to resemble him or herself, known as a Mii. Miis are customizable and allow the participants to capture a caricature likeness of themselves, or others (Fig. 6.2).

Sixteen people participated in the experiment and all experienced all conditions. After they had played each game in the various conditions, the participants filled out a questionnaire regarding their feelings of presence and self-presence. The questionnaire consisted of 28 questions, which correspond to six factors that are correlated with the experience of presence and self-presence: Awareness, Immersion, Involvement, Naturalness, Realness, and Self-presence. We partially based this on the presence questionnaire published by Witmer and Singer in 1998 (see Hoshi and Waterworth 2009, for details).

As expected, there was a significantly higher sense of presence when using a tool versus no tool for both first and third person perspectives ($p < 0.005$, paired T-test). But there was no significant effect on presence of playing from a first person versus a third person perspective for either tool or no tool. There was also no effect on presence of playing with an avatar similar versus dissimilar to self. There was, however, a highly significant increase in self-presence when playing with an avatar similar to self versus dissimilar to self ($p < 0.001$, paired T-test), but no effect of playing with a tool versus no tool.

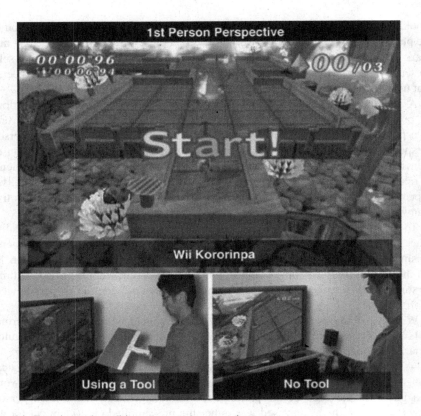

Fig. 6.1 Experimental conditions: 1st person perspective

These results confirm the importance of incorporating tangible tools in blended reality spaces aimed at eliciting a high sense of presence, and also suggest that tangibility has no effect on self-presence. Although a first person perspective is of course more natural than a third person perspective on one's own actions, it did not increase presence, which is a surprising and important finding for the future of blended reality spaces. In fact this suggestion is consistent with some findings (Ehrsson 2007; Lenggenhager et al. 2007) from experimentation on 'out-of-body' experiences (essentially, third person viewpoint experiences of self) supporting the possibility of some kind of 'distributed embodiment' (Waterworth and Waterworth 2014) in blended reality space.

Using a racket is, of course, the natural way to play tennis. In the blended game situation, the physical racket seems to work to bridge the gap between the physical world and virtual world, and increased the feeling of presence. It could be argued that if a game environment does not require such a physical tool, the effects of tangibility on presence may be lacking. While this was not tested in our experiment, we would emphasis that tangibility is not the same as tool-ness. Even in a game

Fig. 6.2 Experimental conditions: 3rd person perspective

where there is no obvious tool – say, a running game – if the game player feels uphill resistance, wind movement, and so on, as physical forces, then tangibility will have been achieved and a high degree of presence can be expected.

The similarity of the virtual representation to the person playing the game strongly affected self-presence, but did not affect presence. Ratan et al. (2007) have also found that participants who used a Mii dissimilar to themselves reported significantly less self-presence than participants who used a Mii similar to themselves, and that feelings of presence were unaffected by character assignment. In fact, presence and self-presence appear to be quite unrelated phenomena. The latter may be more important for social presence than individual presence, which suggests a tension in providing for both – but also gives hints for a nuanced approach to design.

The results have contributed to the design and implementation of strategic combinations of tools, perspectives and avatars for other application scenarios, for example in a design approach to developing free movement based interactions for motor rehabilitation (see below) as well as blended reality spaces for collaboration between hospitals, care organizations and the home.

Physiotherapy for Children

The approach and findings from experiments with blended reality games as described above can be applied to the development of many HCI designs that integrate reality-based touch and force feedback technique into a media environment, most obviously for sports and other training and such medical application areas as remote motor rehabilitation, remote therapy for mental health disabilities, and also collaborative care management for professional staff. Here we consider the design of blended reality spaces for the rehabilitation of children with sensorimotor disorders as an illustrative example.

During the period of a children's rehabilitation at his/her home, professionals and the children already routinely meet via the Internet to discuss the current progress, next collaborative steps and plans for the future. Various crucial decisions are made on the basis of these collaborations. But currently, no satisfactory tools exist to assist in making the right decision, no visualizations or other media representations are brought to assist in these healthcare collaborations. One potential approach is to design and develop intrinsic information devices of various kinds and which also function as multi-sensory interaction devices that can be used in combination within a computerized communication environment (Fig. 6.3). In this blended reality space, tangible interaction objects would be used in four different roles: (i) as input devices, (ii) as user representations, (iii) as system agents, and (iv) as characters in the collaboration. The tangible objects help to create a sense of shared reality between users in different physical places.

Three ways of enhancing immersive and tangible presence in blended reality space can be considered: *Active participation*, *natural flow of action*, and *embodied interaction* (Waterworth and Riva 2014):

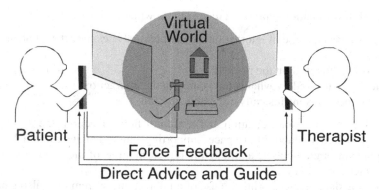

Fig. 6.3 Users at remote sites cooperatively collaborate on rehabilitation by using the object in four different roles

To support active participation, the object is utilized as a user representation medium that allows a user to be a performer and to tell stories by using the object – which then works as a 'living' organism within the blended space and thus between physical locations. The shared collaboration space provides appropriately immersive events where the performers can become emotionally and intellectually involved.

Immersive tasks provided for the children are developed as a blended reality space, which includes various sound and visual effects. It could be a building block experience or telling a story of how to build a house, for example. The auditory and visual representations work as guides for how to achieve children's goals. Executed performances are observed and measured by the system, and can then be processed into representations of achievement and levels of impairment.

Active participation arises from the way the participant plays a role as a performer in an interactive event. If the performer becomes emotionally and intellectually engaged by the events, high levels of presence can arise in the blended reality space.

By picking up, moving, turning, squeezing and in other ways acting on tangible objects, communication with the computer environment and, through it, with other people, can be achieved much more easily. Contextual Information is communicated back via displayed changes to the objects, such as their colour, brightness, vibrations, and the sounds they make. The performer then finds the process of interaction less abstract, more fun, and a much richer and more interesting sensory experience.

Feedback of forces from a physical object provides a sense of touching the virtual object. Variable forces on virtual objects help with rehabilitation that adapts to different levels of impairment. The therapists give more appropriate advice through collaboratively controlling the tangible object with the children. This gives a sense of being together with each other to both therapists and children.

Natural flow of action represents the extent to which:

* There is direct a sense of interaction with contextual cues over the game initiated events,
* Attention is focused on the present,
* Curiosity is aroused by what is happening in the interaction,
* The interaction is intrinsically enjoyable and fun.

Building on active participation and a natural flow of action, the system can provide a shared collaboration space supporting embodied interaction between participants through dynamic and tangible representations of the collaborators and shared objects in real time.

Gathering data by monitoring the use of an object, the system may also generate a visual representation of children's states. The visual information can often be displayed in the periphery of users' attention (Plaue et al. 2004). The peripheral display will then function as a secondary information system while professionals create primary visualizations such as diagnosis or treatment plans.

Through the process of carrying out immersive tasks, gathered data are logged and accumulated in a database. Both therapists and children can access the data easily by interpreting visual representations of it. While the children contribute from a remote site, the visual representation helps the therapists to follow and analyse the circumstances simultaneously. Visually represented improvements in their performance may help to increase their self-confidence, and may help to keep up motivation and active participation in the immersive environment. This approach should make collaborative rehabilitation more effective, by bridging the reality gap between physical and virtual spaces and also between different participants' perceptions in different contexts.

A prototype system has been developed (Sandlund et al. 2009), again using the Nintendo Wii gaming environment, adapted with an additional tangible input object to support the use of more delicate hand movements of the device (to guide a marble through virtual mazes). The target application is for for rehabilitation of children with sensorimotor disorders, and especially for children with cerebral palsy. To achieve this, an accelerometer from inside a Wiimote controller was removed and embedded in various shapes that the child manipulates in specified ways to achieve actions within a game scenario and in the process improve their fine motor skills (see Fig. 6.4).

There is great potential in further work to develop nuanced approaches and methods for assessing motor skills in rehabilitation, and training generally. The goal of the rehabilitation of children with sensorimotor disorders is often not to achieve functional improvements in a short time, especially not if impairment is congenital (Sandlund et al. 2009). The system must capture small changes in motor control by monitoring motor development sensitively over a longer period. We also need to understand and implement mechanisms to interweave information from appropriate contextual aspects of activities. For example, therapists need quantitative information about body parts activated during the play, type of movements, range of movement, movement speed, eye-hand interaction, and endurance measures so on.

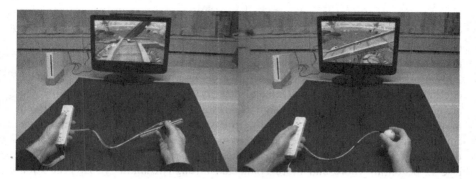

Fig. 6.4 Prototype physical rehabilitation game with two different tangible interaction devices

Practical research work based on experimentation needs to be carefully planned and executed with the prototype. The design and development should also be conducted with all participants over the period in an iterative cycle including design, use, evaluate and modifying the whole system before final implementation.

A Blended Reality Space for Socially Isolated Older People

The human-experiential design approach is ideally suited for age-related critical situations. Park (1992) has described age-related decline in cognitive function. For example, elderly people often have difficulties utilising explicit knowledge and working memory for tasks such as understanding texts, making inferences, encoding information into memory, and retrieving information from memory. In contrast, other mental processes show little or no decline with age. Recent notable approaches to this issue have tried to improve cognitive function by exploiting intact cognitive process such as implicit memory (Ballesteros and Reales 2004, Ballesteros et al. 2007, 2009), which refers to "memories from prior experiences revealed by performance effects in the absence of deliberate recollection" (Zacks et al. 2010, p.305). Elderly people with mild cognitive impairment and dementia still retain concrete implicit skills even if they lose explicit, abstract knowledge and skills. They are still capable of using and being influenced by their past knowledge, whether they are aware of it or not. This is an automatic or unconscious form of memory (Schacter 1987). They have knowledge that their bodies physically remember, as it were, but explicit sources of knowledge such as a user's manual, verbal assistance, and so on, are unsuitable for them.

Designing simple and adequate representations for peripheral media using tangible objects is a key part of developing better combinations of the physical and virtual for this group. The tangible object in the system plays a role to wake up implicit memory in which previous experiences support the performance of a task without conscious awareness of those previous experiences. It has to be designed to link an everyday object and activity that humans remember, for example, how to place fingers on a coffee mug or knot a tie, without consciously thinking about these activities.

Increased mobility means that people's family members and friends may be widely dispersed across geographic distances. This has brought about the situation that elderly people in modern societies are increasingly liying alone and may be insufficiently stimulated, both physically and psycho-socially (Waterworth et al. 2009a). This may then accelerate cognitive decline, creating a vicious circle of decline and reduced social and mental activity. More and more elderly people are suffering loneliness and confusion as a result (Waterworth et al. 2009b). Even though appropriate technology could help ease these problems, older people are actually largely ignored in the design of new information and communication technology, which further contributes to their isolation in a world where everyone else is becoming more and more connected through technology. This situation brings serious concerns and negative impacts not only on elderly people but also on those caring for the elderly, such as family members and health service staff. The potential of new interactive technologies to maintain health and independent living could in principle also improve some cognitive functions in the elderly. Yet only a limited number of experiments have been conducted. What are missing are designs for common technologies that can be used by all people, including the very old, and this is where human-experiential design could have a key role to play.

One trend in recent healthcare is the transfer of nursing care from traditional hospitals to the patient's home. Elderly people are increasingly treated and taken care of in their own homes. But health services cannot keep up with the demand for home visits and day-care. This puts new types of demand on the staff and increases the importance of well functioning communication and collaboration between elderly people at home, care persons, and close family and friends in order to give better health care.

The needs of secondary end users (the carers of the old people) should be considered carefully, but the focus on the elderly as primary user has to be kept central. The primary users could, for example, be provided with a user-sensitive ICT-based home environment that supports a personalized care process by detecting, communicating, and meaningfully responding to relevant states, situations, and activities of the user. So the users might enhance their mental and physical wellbeing with the ICT-based home environment. It should be possible to prevent and manage chronic conditions such as cognitive impairment or dementia by gentle and consistent social stimulation and timely response to detected states, situations or activities, all via appropriately designed technology and communication networks.

Secondary users caring for the elderly, such as family members or close friends would need to actively connect to the network and access information on the person's wellbeing and activities (if approved by the elderly) to get a picture of the elderly person's state and to allow for a much better tailored and timely response, attention and care.

Figure 6.5 is a schematic outline of our approach in the AGNES project (Peter et al. 2013): a context-sensitive home-based interactive system, in which humans utilize background information from ambient media and by means of tangible objects without being disrupted in their foreground tasks.

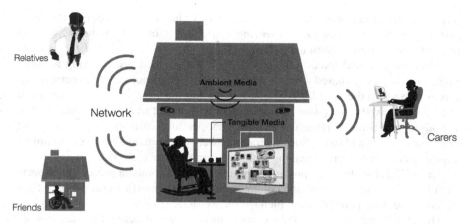

Fig. 6.5 AGNES: a context-sensitive home-based interactive system

This system is composed of ambient displays, tangible interaction objects and interaction mechanisms and protocols, including gesture detection, which makes for easy-to-use and natural interaction. The tangible object and the ambient display complement each other and provide suitably gentle notifications and other information, and establish communication with connected persons. The human focusing of attention between background and foreground has to be a smooth transition, which makes it possible to achieve a natural flow of actions without awareness. Commonly available technologies such as cameras, motion sensors, and mobile devices are used in order to develop cost effective systems for daily use. Sensors should not be intrusive for the target users. By detecting the users' states and activities, the system develops appropriate algorithms to classify mood from facial expressions (Waterworth et al. 2009b). Elderly people living at home also use the system actively by accessing information, sending messages or requesting services.

In AGNES, ambient displays combined with tangible objects in a person's home form a blended reality space, comprising a radically new way to manage social interaction for the elderly. There should be little difference, or ideally no difference, between action/interaction in the blended reality space and ordinary unmediated action in the physical world. Below we outline some of the human-experiential design aspects that were implemented in the project.

Blending Ambient Displays and Tangible Objects

In everyday life, we pick up natural sources of ambient information to understand how things are around us. For example, people can experientially interpret implicit information from outside a window. A subtle combination of brightness, wind direction and humidity gives us the feeling of coming rain. The perceptual feeling of a peaceful curtain-wave may make people feel placid, or people may foresee a storm when they see their curtain waving in the dim light of the window, with no explicit information or conscious effort.

Wind has physical force. As Johnson (1987) mentioned, the meaning of force relies on commonly shared structures that come out from our bodily experience of forces. We grasp the world around us, namely the meaning of 'wind force' from everyday life experiences. Our bodies interact with wind forces that are made up of various natural conditions such as humidity, temperature, darkness/brightness, wind directions, smells and so on. Such interactions between humans and the environment expose recurrent patterns. Meaning structures grow out of such patterns.

The AGNES system can provide a variety of ambient media presenting aspects such as sound, light, airflow, and colour as background interfaces (at the periphery of human sensory perception) in blended reality space (Fig. 6.6).

The elderly person connected to others through social networking technology receives information about messages or stories from family members and others transformed into a variety of ambient forms. For example, the combination of subtle wind and a green light implies notifications coming from family members, mid-level breeze and an orange light means important information has arrived, and strong wind and a vivid red light indicates an urgent message for them.

The ambient display is built on the basis of the blending framework previously discussed (see Fig. 6.7). First, there is a cross-space mapping consisting of two conceptual inputs: input space 1 is explicit information with current technology-based information displays such as voice/text messages, state-activity reports and notifications. The other, input space 2, comprises natural sources in everyday life with their sounds, light, airflow, breeze and shadow. Second, the generic space implies some more abstract structure shared by the inputs. Third, blended reality space, a fourth space, is a new emergent structure that provides tangible presence with no conscious effort of access to information.

Now imagine a situation in the physical world, where an elderly person needs to ask questions of his or her relatives or neighbours. The elderly person may lay a hand on the relative's shoulder, or may knock on a neighbour's door. The tapping and knocking have various meanings, derived from experiences with forces. If it is an emergency situation, they may strongly tap relatives or may knock on the door severely. The meaning of forces includes patterns of embodied experience that obtain through such sensual experiences as the way of our perception, the act of orienting, the interaction with objects, events, and people.

We sense, interpret and codify various patterns, and understand the meaning of forces in a particular situation. The embodied patterns become shared cultural modes in a particular culture (Johnson 1987). The contextual cues on the surface of the AGNES tangible object provide access to implicit memory (Fig. 6.8). The object affords tapping to contact a loved one. We need to carefully choose contextual cues suited to various situations, wood texture to afford knocking, boa material to afford stroking and knit material to afford tapping, based on everyday life objects.

The tangible objects are also built on the basis of the blending design framework (see Fig. 6.9). Input space 1 is that of sensor-based information input techniques

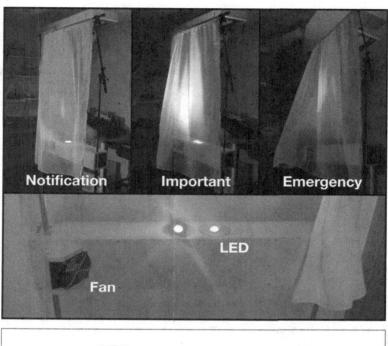

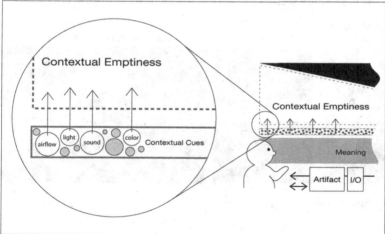

Fig. 6.6 Ambient display in AGNES

such as motion tracking, position tracking and physiological detection. The other, input space 2, is physical activities in everyday life such as tapping, shaking, knocking, and stroking. Here, literal and figurative expressions are established.

Information is breeze from a window
  Communication is tapping someone (memory)

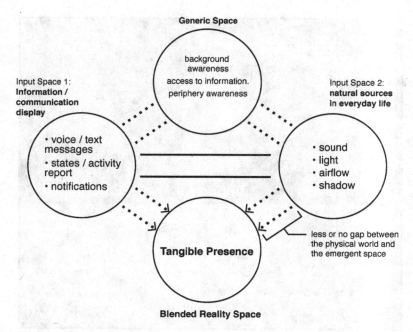

Fig. 6.7 Ambient display as blend

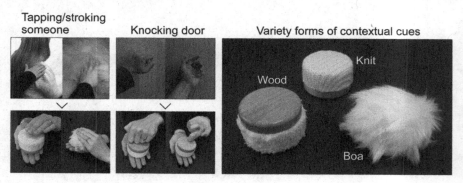

Fig. 6.8 Tangible objects in AGNES

These expressions help us understand information and communication in terms of natural sources/physical activities in everyday life, where there is some similarity or correlation between them. Users understand meaning in their bodily interaction with the world, physically, socially, and culturally.

To ensure user-driven development of the prototypes, users were repeatedly involved in order to collect qualitative data, impressions and opinions by interview and discussion. Their involvement helped iteratively to develop requirement specifications by engaging in testing and evaluating implemented components and the

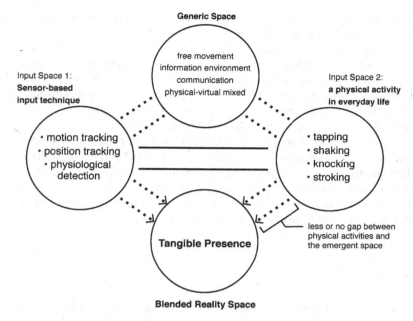

Fig. 6.9 Tangible object as blend

developed prototype system (Peter et al. 2013). The collected information supports the validity of our approach to provide a better fit with the actual needs of our user group. Since this project brought together ten partners from six countries, focus group interviews were conducted in several countries. These revealed interesting feedback and patterns of responses, but not much variance between the three countries (Donetti 2011). The richness of users' impressions gathered by the focus groups helps to trace a clear and consistent picture of issues for the system design, contributing appropriately to development of the system for the particular target users.

In all countries, participants appreciated the limited functionality and simplicity of the ambient display and the tangible object. But they commonly commented on the fact that the tangible object might be lost, and wondered what might happen if they dropped it and it rolled away. From this, they discussed alternative shapes that would be easier to grasp and would not roll. For example, the users mentioned the stiffness in their hands. Shapes like kidneys or dog bones were proposed as good for grasping with their hands. They were also concerned about the fact that they must stay at home in order to get the messages/information. They were afraid of missing some important notifications if they were out. They also suggested other ways based on everyday objects that they would be able to take with them when they left their homes, such as bracelets and keys, which seemed both more discrete and less likely to be left behind. They also considered the need for complementary use of the prototypes with the telephones and wrist alarms that some of them have been using already in their everyday life. These suggestions provide valuable information in the development of improved tangible objects.

The aspects related to sensual perception, such as wood, soft fabric and even the breeze, were also appreciated. In contrast to using current mobile phones, such simplified interaction methods as tapping and knocking were for the most part appreciated by them. All seemed to be very curious about the ambient display. They generally liked the lights and breeze, but questioned whether it would be possible to differentiate the various colours from one another. Sound as an alternative was put forward and this has been adopted for later versions. Their comments also suggested that the ambient display should be installed in an appropriate location at their home for them to effectively sense and recognize the implicit information conveyed. The quality of fabric material for displaying the implicit information is very critical in order to let them use their sensory perception. Such user-led innovation is an absolutely key part of the experiential design approach.

References

Ballesteros S, Reales J (2004) Intact haptic priming in normal aging and Alzheimer's disease: evidence for dissociable memory systems. Neuropsychologia 42(8):1063–1070

Ballesteros S, Reales J, Mayas J (2007) Picture priming in aging and dementia. Psicothema 2:239–244

Ballesteros S, Gonzalez M, Mayas J, Reales JM, Garcia B (2009) Crossmodal object priming in young and older adults: multisensory processing in vision, touch, and audition. Eur J Cogn Psychol Aging Cogn Neurosci 21(2,3):366–387

Becker B, Mark G (2001) Social conventions in computer-mediated communication: a comparison of three online shared virtual environments. In: Schroeder R (ed) The social life of avatars. Springer, London

Borberg M, Piippo P, Ollila E (2008) Designing avatars. In: Proceedings of the 3rd international conference on Digital Interactive Media in Entertainment and Arts (DIMEA'08), Athens, Greece, 2008. ACM, New York

Castranova E (2003) Theory of the avatar. from CESifo: http://papers.ssrn.com/sol3/papers.cfm? abstract_id=385103

Donetti L (2011). Ambient display and tangible interaction to support elderly people: the AGNES project and its possible evolution. Master Thesis, Universita' Degli Studi di Milano – Bicocca, Faculty of Psychology and Mathematics, Physics and Natural Sciences

Ehrsson HH (2007) The experimental induction of out-of-body experiences. Science 317(5841):1048

Hoshi K, Waterworth JA (2009) Tangible presence in blended reality space. Paper presented at the 12th annual international workshop on presence. International Society for Presence Research, Los Angeles

Ishii H (2008) Tangible bits: beyond pixels. Paper presented at the The 2nd international conference on tangible and embedded interaction, ACM press, Kingston

Ishii H, Ullmer B (1997) Tangible bits: towards seamless interfaces between people, bits and atoms. Paper presented at the SIGCHI conference on Human factors in computing systems, Atlanta, GA

Johnson M (1987) The body in the mind: the bodily basis of meaning, imagination and reason. University of Chicago Press, Chicago

Lenggenhager B, Tadi T, Metzinger T, Blanke O (2007) Video ergo sum: manipulating bodily self-consciousness. Science 317(5481):1096–1099

Lombard M, Ditton T (1997) At the heart of it all: the concept of presence. J Comput Mediated-Commun. http://onlinelibrary.wiley.com/doi/10.1111/j.1083-6101.1997.tb00072.x/abstract

Park DC (1992) Applied cognitive aging research. In: Craik FIM, Salthouse TA (eds) The handbook of aging and cognition. LEA, Hillsdale, pp 449–493

Peter C, Kreiner A, Schröter M, Kim H, Bieber G, Öhberg F, Hoshi K, Waterworth EL, Waterworth J, Ballesteros S (2013) AGNES: connecting people in a multimodal way. J Multimodal User Interfaces 7(3):229–245

Plaue C, Miller T, Stasko J (2004) Is a picture worth a thousand words?: an evaluation of information awareness displays. Paper presented at the Graphics Interface 2004, ACM press, Waterloo

Ratan R, Cruz MS, Vorderer P (2007) Multitasking, presence & self-presence on the Wii Paper presented at the The 10th annual international workshop on presence 2007, International Society for Presence Research, Barcelona

Sandlund M, Hoshi K, Waterworth EL, Häger-Ross C (2009) A conceptual framework for design of interactive computer play in rehabilitation of children with sensorimotor disorders. Phys Ther Rev 14(5):384–375

Schacter DL (1987) Implicit memory: history and current status. J Exp Psychol Learn Mem Cogn 13:501–518

Ullmer B, Ishii H (2000) Emerging frameworks for tangible user interfaces. IBM Syst J 39(3):915–931

Waterworth JA, Riva G (2014) Feeling present in the physical world and in computer-mediated environments. Palgrave Macmillan, Basingstoke. ISBN 978-1-13743-166-0

Waterworth JA, Waterworth EL (2008) Presence in the future. International Society for Presence Research. Padova, Italy

Waterworth JA, Waterworth EL (2014) Altered, expanded and distributed embodiment: the three stages of interactive presence. In Riva, Waterworth, Murray D (eds) Interacting with presence: HCI and the sense of presence in computer-mediated environments. De Gruyter Open, Warsaw, Poland

Waterworth JA, Ballesteros S, Peter C (2009a) User-sensitive home-based system for successful ageing. Paper presented at the 2nd international conference on human system interaction, Catania, pp 542–545

Waterworth JA, Ballesteros S, Peter C, Bieber G et al (2009b) Ageing in a networked Society – social inclusion and mental stimulation. Presentation at Workshop on Affect and Behaviour Related Assistance in Support for the Elderly, Corfu, Greece, June 2009

Zacks JM, Speer NK, Swallow KM, Maley CJ (2010) The brain's cutting-room floor: segmentation of narrative cinema. Front Hum Neurosci 4:168. doi:10.3389/fnhum.2010.00168

Chapter 7
Acting and Interacting in the Here and Now

Abstract The final chapter sums up and concludes the book. The future blending of our perceptions of, and actions in, the physical world and through digital technology is not a luxury – it is a necessity. We summarise our view of how to design for the human beings we all are, to support action and interaction in blended reality spaces, and offer predictions about future applications in everyday life. We also provide an overview of the key features, and some limitations of blended reality spaces.

Introduction

In the previous chapter (Chap. 6), we presented in some detail how the human-experiential design approach can be applied to create blended reality spaces for particular purposes, including interactive games and a home support and communication system for the elderly. In this chapter we offer predictions about future applications in everyday life, allowing people to live in the here and now while feeling present and acting in a seamlessly blended combination of the physical world and digital information and communication channels. We also provide an overview of the key features, advantages and some limitations of our approach to designing blended reality spaces.

In recent years digital technology has addressed and changed several different aspects of our daily life and work. These aspects include our mental activities, such as how we remember things and find our way in new environments. For example, we need no longer carry out mental arithmetic, memorise phone numbers, or study maps in advance to find our way in a city we are visiting for the first time. These things are dealt with by technology and so we no longer need do this work. Our bodies, too, benefit from the new technologies that tell us how many calories we are using, how many steps we have taken today, whether we are exercising too little or too much. Our social lives have also been transformed by the use of mobile phones, text messaging and social media, with very few individuals choosing not to be connected with people they know (and many they don't really know) in this way.

We increasingly live in a world of mixed realities. Through the proliferation of personal mobile devices and possibilities for ubiquitous computing, we almost constantly interact with digital content and communications often while also navigating

© Springer International Publishing Switzerland 2016
J. Waterworth, K. Hoshi, *Human-Experiential Design of Presence in Everyday Blended Reality*, Human–Computer Interaction Series, DOI 10.1007/978-3-319-30334-5_7

in physical space. Our mental lives have been split between two intertwined, but not as yet integrated, realities: the physical and the digital. Social interaction is similarly split, we struggle to manage our encounters with distant others brought to us via technology while trying to simultaneously fulfill the social expectations of those in our current physical vicinity.

We have suggested that a key aspect of our experience of the world, of both the physical and technology-mediated environments, is our *sense of presence* – the feeling of being in the here and now. The here and now is always where we are present. We can only act, and interact, with intention when we are present, and so we seek to be psychologically and socially present both in the physical and the digital world of networked communications. And we can only feel our own presence in an external environment when we have the potential to act – or interact – even if we intentionally choose not too. Since presence is an attention-demanding state, and because these worlds are mixed but not yet integrated, this is a troublesome and sometimes dangerous task. Our sense of presence has been split between the physical and digital worlds we inhabit. Moment by moment we must decide which reality to prioritize, and how and when to switch between the two becomes a major concern throughout our everyday lives.

Designing for Humans

We stressed two points in addressing the problem identified in the last paragraph. The first point concerned the importance of taking account of universal primitives underlying the way people understand things, events, relationships – and information generally. By this view, because we are all embodied biological beings, meaning ultimately resides in bodily experiences. Our bodies and minds have evolved to act in the physical world, and how we are able to understand any information is derived from that. If we design for this embodiment, understandability should follow. And since we all share the same evolutionary history and hence, bodily structures and potential for experiences, we share the same primitives for understanding information. This is what makes social interaction possible. If we design for embodiment in the right way, the potential for shared understanding should also follow, even between people who exist in different contexts.

The second point concerns taking account of the importance of an integrated sense of presence, which would makes it possible for us to carry out our intentions and act in any world in which we find ourselves in the here and now. These points, which can be seen as different aspects of the problems of humans acting in current mixed realities, are also key part of the design solution. Together, they form the basis for what we call in the book human-experiential design, which we claim make possible the design of effective mixed realities – blended reality spaces. Blended reality spaces have the potential to bridge the contextual and perceptual gaps between the digital and the physical, and the proximal and the distant, and provide an integrated sense of presence underlying intentional action and interaction.

Human-experiential design is an approach rooted in a return to first principles of how people understand the world, consciously and unconsciously, and how this determines the way they think, act, and communicate. Humans' implicit knowledge as embodied in everyday life activities comes out in our unconscious motor behaviour, such as the way we use a chair, hold a coffee mug, turn a doorknob, and feel the saddle of a bicycle. We are not aware of these as particular objects or behaviours, but we are unconsciously harmonious with them. The objects themselves disappear from our perception. The design is silent or only perceived later. So users need not read user manuals, need not understand explicit conceptual information to act.

The embodied patterns repeatedly developed in everyday life merge when action and meaning are integrated in a particular situation. The design image that the designer forms of a solution is thought to be subjective and embodied in the designer. But if the designer's embodied image is shared in an image embodied in users, they should empathize with the feeling provoked by it. The human-experiential designer needs to focus images that people commonly might embody, so that they feel empathic towards the design.

It is important to focus on people's natural flow of actions during user observations. It is not always easy to find the embodied patterns or primitives that affect the sense of flow, of mentally effortless action, because they exist pervasively and predominantly at a pre-conceptual level. Ironically, the natural flow of action occurs when we are unconscious of our actions. We usually cannot conceive an embodied idea consciously. More problematic still is the fact that user observation and other applied user research consciously intends to analyse and evaluate users. Observed and tested users may even provide comments from a 'user's' point of view – not as the people they are in everyday life.

In order to conduct user research in a way that will succeed in terms of human-experiential design, certainly principles need to be observed.

- First, all research participants should be encouraged to divest themselves of identity labels such as designer, user, and researcher.
- Second, the designer has to be embodied in the user's experience, meaning that the participants need to carefully investigate how the embodied image that the designer forms can be shared with the image users form from their own experiences.
- Third, the embodied patterns have to be outlined by introspecting about everyday life, since the participants share the same human primitives. The participants need to pay attention so whether the designed things are embedded into their experience or not, because the design should penetrate into their everyday life in a way that does not break their natural flow of action.

We see human-experiential design not as an activity that makes users satisfied by experiences, but as something that, rather, modestly seeks to disappear from users' perception. While 'doing design' is a particular subjective, imaginative and embodied action for a designer, 'describing design' must be general in character since description expresses what is common across different objects and situations.

For example, the description 'coffee mug' can be applied to all mug-style cups and defines what mug-style cups share in common that specifies them as 'coffee mug'. 'Describing design' is not a particular image of design as one thing or another. Whereas 'doing design' is tied to the particular mind that experiences a designer's embodied images, 'describing design' is disembodied in the sense that it is shareable, abstract, and of a general nature.

These days, users hardly empathize with design even though they may speak of well-designed products. The particular subjective and embodied images that the designer forms are converted into products or artefacts targeted for the general and abstract nature of a defined class of customers. It is disembodied design expressed as explicit information shared by customers in a potential segmentation of the market.

Whereas design for a particular group based on segmentation variables shares the general and abstract nature of information, human-experiential design shares pre-conceptual and embodied primitives. This is because our bodies are tied to the world around us, and our imagination and rationality are inseparable from bodily orientations and interactions with the environment that all humans must have experienced to be human. We see this is the route to true universal design inclusive of design for a particular group of people.

Acting and Interacting in the Here and Now

The future blending of our perceptions of, and actions in, the physical world and through digital technology is not a luxury – it is a necessity. Mixing realities is causing a disintegration of social life since we may be in the same physical space as others, but with each person personally engaged with a distant other. Parents pushing prams seem close to their children, but the physical proximity may belie a communicative absence, as they are engaged with absent others via their mobile phones.

The question of life-work balance is also important. People separate, integrate, or hop between private life and work. Integration is hindered by the current nature of technology – one switches attention between the here (of a movie, say) and the there (of e-mails, say), when trying to relax on the sofa and attend to both – perhaps with a glass in hand. There is a current trend to use techniques such as mindfulness training to attend to the present moment, but current technology breaks this focus (The Psychologist 2015).

Blended reality spaces can support an integration of such diverse aspects, so that an unbroken focus on the present moment could include a movie, e-mail, and even social media. Existing views of presence have focused either on the sense of being in the physical world, or that of being in the digital – immersed in media – which is generally referred to as mediated presence. Blended reality spaces brings together the current physical space, the person and things located there, and physically distant other people and places. The sense of presence – quintessentially about being attentionally and intentionally located in the physical and temporal present –

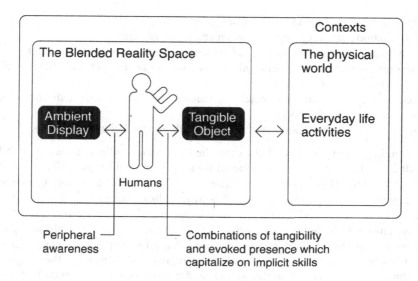

Fig. 7.1 Acting in the here and now in blended reality space

becomes *blended presence*, which encompasses other people and places within the human sense of here and now. The technology has become part of the self, and the blended reality space to which we are attending has become an integrated part of the non-self, the world around the self.

The general principle is that a blended reality space is designed to take account of human characteristics and the context of use to provide an integrated sense of blended presence in a physical/virtual environment. This sense of blended presence supports and is characterised by effective action in the blended reality space. Acting and interacting become one and the same. Figure 7.1 shows this in simplified form.

In Fig. 7.1, "ambient displays" represent a range of possible display media, including augmented reality glasses, large-scale displays in public places or other physical spaces, auditory displays via headphones, tangible displays including vibrations, music, voice or other sounds emitted by physical objects. On the input side, "tangible objects" stands for the whole range of physical objects that can provide inputs by virtue of their position in space, geographical location, state or other contextual information and including the user's bodily state. These, combined with the surrounding physical environment and the activities being undertaken there, comprise the context. Based on inputs from sensors and the behaviours of the user, his or her relative sense of presence between virtual and physical aspects of the blend can be dynamically adjusted to achieve an appropriate *balance* for the individual user.

We foresee a range of personal environments that centre on mobile and wearable technologies. Through the use of augmented reality and ambient displays, and integrated with carried and worn sensor-based inputs from the user, a blended personal reality space could in principle support a wide range of possible functionalities including:

- Navigation and orientation in physical space
- Information pull according to location and personal state
- Connectivity to others with tailored presence according to tracked context
- Automatic exchange of personal information along pre-set and dynamically selected parameters
- Receptivity to personally-targeted push announcements, based on similar selection and geographical location
- State dependent entertainment, integrated with personal communications

Extending from the essentially embodied use case outlined about, a mobile blended reality space would provide additional functionality and information as necessary for travel via a personal vehicle or public modes of transport. On-screen augmented reality displays, coupled with tactile feedback through the steering wheel and other vehicle surfaces, could provide appropriate display possibilities. Inputs to the system could include motion sensors, eye-tracking devices and physiological sensors to capture driver/passenger state, in addition to explicit controls such as tangible objects (switches, dials) and voice inputs. In addition to the range of functionalities listed above, traffic, vehicle and environmental data would form part of the ambient environment. Mechanisms for dynamic balancing would be needed to cater for emergencies and other changing circumstances, as well as for personal characteristics and preferences of specific users.

Personal blended reality spaces could also interact with public spaces equipped with appropriate sensing and communication infrastructures. These would include ambient and other displays, sensing of participant locations and activities, amongst other features. Everyday events such as buying groceries, filling a car with fuel, or paying for parking space would simply require actions in physical space, and these would also enact intentions executed in the virtual realm – most importantly payment transactions – since aspects of the physical world will be dynamically identified within the current blended reality space. There would be no need for credit or other payment cards, or mixed reality methods (such as sending a specific mobile phone messages to particular phone numbers).

In Conclusion

Human-experiential design of physical-digital materials and environments has the potential to impact on our lives in several different but ultimately interrelated ways.

Our mental activities will be changed along with some of the ways in which we carry out our intentions. An integrated sense of mediated presence can potentially provide a smoother link between our intentions and actions in mixed reality.

The way in which we perceive and function with our bodies – our sense of our own embodiment – will also be changed, when we perceive ourselves acting from the altered perspectives provided by technology. Everyday perception of the physical world will be augmented with overlaid and intertwined computer-generated sights and sounds, but the individual experience will remain that of presence in a changed physical world – a world where physical acts also accomplish intention in the virtual sphere. In blended reality spaces – which also include parts of the immediate physical world – our bodies will have altered powers of perception and action.

The widespread transformation of our social lives with technology is ongoing and ever expanding. This can lead to a reduction in our sense of the reality of others, but also and conversely to the situation in which we share more information with others than ever before, and in ways that were previously impossible. How and in what respects we are aware of others should depend on the contextual situation in which we find ourselves. Some community-based systems provide an example of how presence can be carefully designing into social participation systems, for example through the use of telepresence robots, and can provide a kind of social presence ('*hyperpresence*') that exceeds the natural in some respects (Carroll et al. 2014). The digital transformation of physical places is another product of designed mixed reality spaces, both through architectural installations and through mobile and wearable devices.

Blends of the proximal and the distal already occur in some situations, such as those provided by videoconferencing systems. As of now, these happen in specific physical places. But the trend towards mobile media access seems inevitable, and we can anticipate mediated meetings of physically distant and proximal people, each experiencing a consistent blended physical-virtual reality including all participants. For this to work, media devices will need to be sensitive to both the situational context of their use, and the state of their users. Presence levels will be adjusted dynamically during the management of blended streams of incoming and outgoing information.

Technology creates the virtual world, but also exists in the physical world – with which the virtual often competes for our attention. From an idealistic viewpoint, in a true blending of the physical and the virtual, the technology itself should completely disappear from our perception. In such a situation, there will be no conscious effort of access to information (Waterworth and Waterworth 2010). It would then be possible to realize an ideal in which our activities are characterized by a natural flow of action, without any intrusion from technology, from the physical-virtual divide. Like a fish in a clear stream, a high-skilled player playing with an immersive, interactive and body-movement oriented computer game shows a clear example of little or no conscious effort of access to information. The user perceives and acts directly, in everyday life unmediated activities.

The human-experiential approach is a viable approach to the creation of everyday blended reality. It does this by focusing on people as humans, each with their own needs and preferences but all sharing universal characteristics. It brings with it the possibility to establish a new disciplinary field merging design with cognitive science, presence research, neuroscience, and HCI research. But this will first require a fresh framework for understanding and manipulating the contextual influences that affect interactive systems and their users. The need to investigate the factors influencing presence in new blended reality spaces will become ever more critical, and new methods of user experience assessment will be needed to fully capitalise on the potential of blended reality spaces.

As we stated at the beginning of the book, technology is constantly changing, but people remain the same. They consciously perceive the world around them, and act out their intentions there, in the present time and place in which they are located. They do this on the basis of evolved bodies and structures of meaning that have remained unchanged over millennia. More than ever before, the here and now reality in which we all live and function is comprised of both physical and virtual elements, but these elements are currently not well integrated and generally interfere with each other. In this book we have presented the human-experiential design of blended reality spaces – interactive spaces that combine the physical and the virtual in ways that match humans sense making and action in the here and now.

References

Carroll JM, Shih PC, Hoffman B, Wang J, Han K (2014). Presence and hyperpresence: implications for community awareness. In: Riva, Waterworth, Murray D (eds) Interacting with presence: HCI and the sense of presence in computer-mediated environments. De Gruyter Open, Warsaw, Poland

The Psychologist, 28, 7, July 2015, page 577

Waterworth EL, Waterworth JA (2010) Mediated presence in the future. In: Bracken CC, Skalski PD (eds) Immersed in media: telepresence in everyday life. Routledge, Taylor & Francis Group, New York, pp 183–196

Author Index

© Springer International Publishing Switzerland 2016
J. Waterworth, K. Hoshi, *Human-Experiential Design of Presence
in Everyday Blended Reality*, Human–Computer Interaction Series,
DOI 10.1007/978-3-319-30334-5

Subject Index

© Springer International Publishing Switzerland 2016
J. Waterworth, K. Hoshi, *Human-Experiential Design of Presence
in Everyday Blended Reality*, Human–Computer Interaction Series,
DOI 10.1007/978-3-319-30334-5

Printed in the United States
By Bookmasters